"Endless admiration and respect for John in writing such an important book on a topic often ignored, a remarkable effort focusing on athletes, not because of their athletic accomplishments, but for the insights on their resolute commitment to their faith that has guided them. John's own faith journey and internal challenges faced while surrounded by so many with a different perspective is forthright and authentic and his frequent use of Bible verses is impactful. You will check your emotions when reading the exchange between Bobby Richardson and Mickey Mantle in the latter's final days. The long wait for this kind of book required an appropriate and skilled person of faith to step forward in due time. That time is now."

—**Tim Mead**, former president of the National Baseball Hall of Fame in Cooperstown, NY

When was the last time a book's introduction gave you a shiver? Mine was when I read the introduction to John Strege's *In the Big Inning*. I defy anyone who is a fan of any sport and a believer, no matter the denomination or depth of faith, to not finish the introduction and to continue reading, maybe for what you might guess is the exchange recounted between Coach Urban Meyer and Tim Tebow, and I will admit that is the sort of story one reads books to collect and keep handy for many conversations. But that isn't it. It's the Rafer Johnson anecdote and that's all I will say. Read it.

I will add that while Strege writes "some players and a manager, familiar names, who emphatically would have argued that" Strege wasn't a good sportswriter, anyone who follows the business knows that's not true. Strege is a master of a difficult art—conveying competition in print—and those he has covered and those he has served know that. What they won't know until they read *In the Big*

Inning is that John came to work every day with an unfair advantage of absolute faith that God was running the show. What an advantage to a writer. To every player and coach. To every reader. Please, if you love sports or God or preferably both, read this. It will change how and why you witness. It will inspire even as it entertains. And it will give you courage for the day ahead.

Thanks to every athlete and coach and manager who spoke to John for this book. It should be a staple of school libraries and locker rooms for years to come and it will teach everyone who reads it never to be ashamed of the Gospel "because it is the power of God to salvation for everyone who believes." Especially if you have to live with winning and losing with audiences large and small watching and judging. Get a second copy and send it to any young man or woman engaged on the fields of play in any sport. They will thank you.

—**Hugh Hewitt,** host of the nationally syndicated *Hugh Hewitt Radio Show*, panelist on Fox News Channel's *Special Report with Bret Baier, Washington Post* columnist, Chapman University law professor, and former assistant White House counsel in the Reagan administration

IN THE BIG INNING

WHERE FAITH MEETS SPORTS:
A CHRISTIAN SPORTSWRITER'S
PERSPECTIVE

JOHN STREGE

MEDIA.COM

Published by
Illumify Media Global
www.IllumifyMedia.com
"Let's bring your book to life!"

Paperback ISBN: 978-1-959099-53-6

Cover design by Debbie Lewis

Printed in the United States of America

For Carl Catlin

Contents

Acknowledgments   ix

Introduction   xi

1. In the Big Inning. . .   1
2. Dusty Baker and the Power of Prayer   11
3. The Tebow Template   21
4. Peach Baskets to Rafer Johnson: The Influencers   32
5. The Elysian Fields   39
6. The Sound-Bite Witness   59
7. Does God Pick Winners?   72
8. Mickey Mantle Goes to Heaven   81
9. Separation of Church and. . . Sports?   88
10. Remember the Sabbath to Keep It. . . What's that Again?   101
11. The Power of One   111
12. Seventeen Inches   116
13. Coaches, Courts, and Controversies   126
14. Now Serving. . .   136
15. Applause is Not the Joyful Noise   142

Notes   149

About the Author   151

Acknowledgments

I have been blessed in my life and long career to have known many Christian men and women who have contributed to helping make me be a better person, admittedly a challenge at times, and I am still a work in progress. One of those men, Carl Catlin, has been a better corner man for me than the great boxing trainer Angelo Dundee was for Muhammad Ali. Carl's Christian leadership, friendship, our shared love of baseball and the Lord (though not in that order), and his support for this project from its inception has meant the world to me. Thank you, Carl.

Paul Batura, vice president of communications at Focus on the Family, is a prolific and talented writer, a great family man and friend, and a strong Christian influence on me, one who graciously allows me to bounce ideas off him. This project would not have happened without his encouragement.

Finally, nothing good happens without a great support system that starts with my wife of, well, a lot of years, Marlene, and our daughter Hannah, who already has helped change the world and will continue to do so in so many good and godly ways. I love you both as big as the sky, as Hannah says.

Introduction

Christianity and sports have been the two constants in my life, one from birth, the other from the time I was old enough to throw and catch a ball. I was baptized at Immanuel Lutheran Church in Everett, Washington, confirmed at Trinity Lutheran Church in Whittier, California, married there, too. I attended Lutheran elementary schools, first through eighth grades, in five different cities, the result of my father frequently having been transferred by his employer.

In order, then: I was a fan of the Seattle Rainiers in the old Pacific Coast League, the St. Louis Cardinals, the Kansas City Athletics, before they moved to Oakland, the Detroit Tigers, and finally, to a lesser degree, the Dodgers and the Angels. My dad was an avid sports fan, to such an extent that on any fall Saturday evening he would search his television for a football game to watch, and he might stumble on, say, Idaho State playing Montana, and quickly would develop a rooting interest. But he especially loved big-time sports, and he had an eager accomplice in me. He took me to the first of two Major League Baseball All-Star Games played in 1960, in Kansas City, where I saw—though do not remember seeing —Ted Williams and Stan Musial pinch hit, Willie Mays play center field, Henry Aaron and Roberto Clemente play right field, and several other Hall of Famers. In 1961, he took me to the old College All-Star Football Game at Soldier Field in Chicago, the Philadelphia Eagles versus the college all-stars. He took me to game three of the 1963 World Series at Dodger Stadium, the Dodgers beating the Yankees, 1-0, and to the 1964 Rose Bowl Game, where his Washington Huskies lost to Illinois, 17-7.

My mother was an English major at what then was called Washington State College (now Washington State University) and was an avid reader who somehow could concentrate on what she was reading even as my father was yelling at the television over a pass dropped by a nameless receiver on the team for which he had decided to root. "You know, they can't hear you," she'd say. More than once. I confess that I am guilty, too, of letting the television know of my displeasure on occasion. My mom bequeathed to me the gift of reading enjoyment. She did not care what I read, so long as I read. I believe I had all twenty-three books in Clair Bee's *Chip Hilton Series*. Bee was a Hall of Fame basketball coach who created Chip Hilton, a young wholesome star in football, basketball, and baseball. These books were great reading, underpinned by moral lessons, for this avid eight-, nine-, and ten-year-old sports fan.

I also had subscriptions to *Baseball Digest* and the *Sporting News* at an early age—and was fortunate to have been a contributor to the latter in the early eighties. I recall at nine or ten years old waking up a few minutes earlier than my dad every morning when we lived in Farmington, Michigan, to beat him to the *Detroit Free Press* sports section. I often fell asleep listening on a small transistor radio to the great Ernie Harwell broadcasting Tigers games. I was fortunate to meet Mr. Harwell many years later when I was a baseball writer, and sat next to him, pre-game, in the Tigers' dugout talking to him for a few minutes, a fanboy with a former idol. He did not disappoint.

It was no surprise, then, given my love of sports, playing them and reading about them, that it led me to a career in sports, though, alas, not as an athlete. I batted .250 in the only year I played varsity baseball for La Serna High in Whittier, California. I also grew up down the street in Whittier from friend Jamie Quirk, who allowed me to see up close what a real athlete looked like. It did not look like me. Quirk was six-foot-four, lean, one of the best high school quarterbacks in the country, who had signed a letter of intent to play for coach Ara Parseghian at Notre Dame. But he also was a first-round draft choice of the Kansas City Royals, opted for baseball and a six-figure signing bonus over football, and eventually played parts of eighteen years in the Major Leagues, followed by decades as a coach in the major leagues and as a minor league manager.

An aside, a story Quirk told me the last time I saw him, when he was managing the San Diego Padres' Class A team, the Lake Elsinore (California) Storm. A year after Quirk had declined Notre Dame's scholarship offer, Joe Montana enrolled at Notre Dame. When Quirk's playing career ended and he returned to the Kansas City Royals as a coach in 1994, Montana by then was playing quarterback for the Kansas City Chiefs. The two were introduced, and Quirk jokingly said that had he opted for football at Notre Dame rather than baseball with the Royals, no one would ever have heard of Montana, who of course became one of the greatest quarterbacks in NFL history.

My own dreams of athletic stardom dashed, I instead combined my love of sports and the written word. I fell into sportswriting as a career, one that eventually spanned more than fifty years, counting high school years stringing for a local newspaper, the *Whittier Daily News*, and including stops at the *Los Angeles Times* and *Orange County Register* newspapers. Since December of 1997, I've been at *Golf Digest* magazine. I am a member of the Golf Writers Association of America and a Lifetime Honorary Member of the Baseball Writers Association of America.

Others can decide whether I was good at my chosen profession, and there were some players and a manager, familiar names, who emphatically would have argued that I wasn't. I'd call that an occupational hazard, but it does not warrant such a designation. I spent one college summer working in a sawmill, Buse Timber, in Everett, Washington, where real occupational hazards existed. I am grateful that I left with all ten fingers intact inasmuch as I would be typing for a living.

But I can say unequivocally that I have not always been good at living out my faith. We are all sinners, of course, hence the reason we recite this confessional in our church on many Sundays:

> I, a poor, miserable sinner, confess unto You all my sins and iniquities with which I have ever offended You and justly deserved Your temporal and eternal punishment. But I am heartily sorry for them and sincerely repent of them, and I pray You of Your boundless mercy and for the sake of the holy, innocent, bitter sufferings and death of Your beloved Son, Jesus Christ, to be gracious and merciful to me, a poor, sinful being.

But it bears reminding here, and always, the good news, our redemption from our sinful nature, encapsulated in a single word, the most important in Christianity: Grace.

"Grace is God's best idea," Max Lucado, the renowned pastor and Christian author, said. "His decision to ravage a people by love, to rescue passionately, and to restore justly—what rivals it? Of all his wondrous works, grace, in my estimation, is the magnum opus."

Paul succinctly summed up the word's importance when he wrote, "For by grace you have been saved through faith" (Ephesians 2:8 ESV).

I am a regular at church, and I doubt that I've ever attended a service in which grace was not mentioned. At the outset of sermons, pastors routinely state the apostle Paul's words in his letters, "Grace and peace to you from God our Father and from our Lord and Savior Jesus Christ, Amen."

Throughout my career I was always attuned to the Christian athletes with whom I came in contact, among them Dusty Baker, the manager of the 2022 World Series-champion Houston Astros, an old friend from my days on the Dodgers beat. I had a forty-minute phone conversation with him, discussing his own faith and prayer life detailed later in this book, and he could have been speaking on behalf of all Christians, starting with me, when he said, "I don't always do what I'm supposed to do. But I know what I'm supposed to do. And you can ask forgiveness." Forgiveness, of course, is dependent on God's grace.

It is these two constants in my life, faith and sports, that long ago piqued my interest in how they have intersected through the years: the questions they've raised; the impact they've had; the controversies they've engendered; their growing importance in an age of declining interest in Christianity; and the opportunities Christian athletes now have to help stem the tide of our Lord and Savior Jesus Christ getting squeezed out on so many fronts, among them the public square and the church pews.

It falls on all Christians to embrace the Great Commission, to "Go therefore and make disciples of all nations, baptizing them in the name of the Father, and of the Son and of the Holy Spirit, teaching them to observe all that I have commanded you. And behold, I am with you always, to the end of the age" (Matthew 28:19–20 ESV). It is especially important that all Christians, but in this case Christian athletes, use the platforms now available to them to follow this decree, to amplify the message of salvation, and many who do so are mentioned in this book.

I am neither a theologian nor a biblical scholar, just a sinful layman who was raised a Christian and was blessed to have had a long background in sports and an interest in exploring the intersection of the two from a variety of angles, while hopefully living up to my responsibility as a Christian to adhere to the Great Commission. And, God willing, to do so in an informative, inspiring, entertaining, and, occasionally, even humorous way.

Yes, there is room for humor in Christianity, to wit LPGA golfer Amy Olson, a devout Christian, who incidentally played in the 2023 U.S. Women's Open while seven months pregnant. Olson tweeted, "You know you are in a Bible study with golfers when they compare the armor David tried on for battle with Goliath to swinging in rain gear." Well played, Amy.

And, finally, Solomon notes that "For everything there is a season, and a time for every matter under heaven. . . a time to weep and a time to *laugh*" (Ecclesiastes 3:1, 4 ESV, emphasis added).

To quote the late great Hall of Fame baseball manager Casey Stengel, "You could look it up."

ONE

In the Big Inning. . .

A SENSE of humor is not a requirement for becoming a man of the cloth, but neither does it hurt. The nineteenth century English preacher Charles Spurgeon once noted that it was "less a crime to cause a momentary laughter than a half-hour's profound slumber." The first rule of the sermon? Keep 'em awake. G. K. Chesterton, the renowned English writer, philosopher, lay theologian, literary critic, and art critic—a five-tool player, to borrow from the vernacular of the baseball scout—offered up the test of a good religion: "Whether you can joke about it," he wrote.

My wife and I have been blessed over the years to have had great pastors, most of them sports fans, and many with keen senses of humor they were not averse to using in otherwise serious homilies about salvation. Fire, brimstone, and comic relief, as it were. Our current pastor, the Reverend Mark Moreno, is a diehard fan of the Chicago Cubs, notwithstanding his being raised in Houston, attending college in Nebraska, and having gone to the seminary in St. Louis. Go figure. The Cubs often turn up in his Sunday morning sermons, usually evoking laughter, often at his own expense. Of course, to be a diehard Cubs fan requires that one has a sense of humor. When the Cubs won the World Series in 2016, it was their first world championship since 1908. For those keeping score at home, as the radio broadcasters say, that's more than a century between titles.

It was in a sermon given by another of our pastors that I first heard the old joke about baseball having been mentioned in the Bible. I am a former baseball writer, who spent time on the Angels and Dodgers beats, the latter when combustible Tommy Lasorda was the manager. Talk about fire, brimstone, and comic relief. More on that later. But any mention of our national pastime from the pulpit immediately gets my attention, not that I was otherwise not paying attention, of course. "It's right there in Genesis 1:1," the pastor said. "In the big inning." Predictably, it evoked both groans and guffaws, while serving a purpose. It got everyone's attention.

I bring this up because Genesis 1:1, "In the beginning. . ." or "In the big inning. . ." as the joke goes, loosely connects the Bible to baseball, seemingly a logical place to begin an examination of the intersection of Christianity and sports. Curious bedfellows, Christianity and sports. Or so one might think. The evidence overwhelmingly says otherwise. This intersection has always been a heavily trafficked one, more so now in the age of social media and expanded television coverage of professional and college sports.

Scottie Scheffler's news conference following his Masters victory in 2022 should serve as a template for all Christian athletes. It's a textbook example of a Christian athlete speaking honestly and from the heart, referencing his faith, without concern how others might perceive it. It began when he was asked how his Sunday morning and early afternoon went as the Masters leader awaiting his late tee time.

"I cried like a baby this morning," he said. "I was so stressed out. I didn't know what to do. I was sitting there telling [wife] Meredith, 'I don't think I'm ready for this. I'm not ready. I don't feel like I'm ready for this kind of stuff,' and I just felt overwhelmed. She told me, 'Who are you to say that you are not ready?' And so what we talked about is that God is in control and that the Lord is leading me, and if today is my time, it's my time. And if I shot eighty-two today, somehow I was going to use it for his glory."

The interview was televised on Golf Channel and was seen and heard by a large audience, though perhaps not as large an audience as that watching on ESPN the Heisman Trophy ceremony from New York City in December, 2021. The Heisman winner was Alabama's poised sophomore quarterback Bryce Young, whose first words in his acceptance speech were these: "First and foremost, I'd like to thank my Lord and Savior, Jesus Christ. Without him, I couldn't be here. Through him, all things are possible."

Philippians 4:13, cited on ESPN before a large national television audience, reminding us that, yes, there is a higher power than Nick Saban, even in the Southeastern Conference.

Bryce Young, though only twenty at the time, showed how it is done, how Christian athletes can use the opportunities available to them to witness for Christ, even in five-second sound bites. The obvious question is whether it has an impact, and the answers I generally get from those I've asked is that it does, by allowing the Holy Spirit to take over from there. "It's helpful for people who might be on the fence [about Christianity]," the estimable baseball man Dusty Baker told me.

Those fences, incidentally, are always crowded.

Christianity and sports both evoke zealotry, and for many fans, sports are a religion. There is no greater place to witness "religious" zealotry than at a Southeastern Conference football game on a fall Saturday afternoon. The former football coach Bill Curry often told the story about his accepting the head coaching position at the University of Alabama in 1987, not a popular move in Tuscaloosa at the time. His pastor, Bill Floyd, phoned his home and spoke with Curry's wife Carolyn, asking if they were okay.

"Of course we are fine," Carolyn said. "You must understand, Bill, that these people are serious about football. To them it is a religion."

"Oh, no, Carolyn," Reverend Floyd replied. "It is a whole lot more important than that."

Religion on steroids.

Christianity, it should not have to be said, though it is imperative that we note it here, is substantially more important than sports. Combining the two, though, can be a force for good. Every game is a stage and an opportunity for Christian athletes to share their faith in following Jesus' command in the Great Commission, to "Go therefore and make disciples of all nations, baptizing them in the name of the Father and of the Son and of the Holy Spirit." The twenty-first century is being live-streamed, its games, matches, and tournaments ubiquitous across televisions and computer screens and cell phones, then dissected endlessly on a variety of media platforms, providing Christian athletes opportunities heretofore unimaginable.

Let Golden State Warriors star Steph Curry be our guide.

"Each game," he once said, "is an opportunity to be on a great stage and be a witness for Christ. When I step on the floor, people should know who I represent, who I believe in."

Christian role models are called—as all Christians are called—to help counter a culture that is ailing. "We need role models," the best-selling Christian author Eric Metaxas said in an interview with Seattle Pacific University's magazine *Response* in 2013. "It's one thing to talk about how we should behave; it's another thing to see it. I think that that's part of why the Wilberforce book and the Bonhoeffer book [biographies Metaxas authored], in particular, have caught on. We don't have a lot of good examples. We have a lot of bad examples. But how *should* you live? What is a heroic life? Dedicated to God, dedicated to truth, and goodness, and justice? What does that look like? We don't have all that many examples of that in the culture. Why?"

Metaxas noted in his interview with *Response*, "I've been thinking this way a number of years: We allow ourselves to be merely religious and stand in a religious corner, when God calls us to be in everything."

Yes, everything, and by us, he means all Christians, including Christian athletes. And even Christian sportswriters.

I spoke with Len Vanden Bos, the team chaplain of the Buffalo

Bills, and asked him about a Christian athlete's obligation to share their faith. "The responsibility of the Christian athlete is to steward, obviously, what he's been given, just like all of us," he said. "None of it is our own. It's what we've been given. They've been given an opportunity and a platform to use for good. There are so many great NFL players that have great causes and do tremendous work in their communities.

"As a Christian athlete, one of those opportunities is to share the gospel, to use the opportunities, whether it be a microphone or out in the community. It's an opportunity for them to give glory to God. I'm on Twitter, and after every game one of our photographers takes a picture of the prayer huddle and I send it out every week, 'To God be glory. Go Bills.'

"These players have so much more of a platform. That's part of discipleship, too. My wife and I disciple these players and couples, to engage how to steward with that they've been given. It's one piece of stewardship, and for a short amount of time, they have a pretty big stage."

Several sports stars, without hesitation, profess their love for the Lord via Twitter (now called X) or a post-game statement, including the NFL's Russell Wilson and retired quarterback Drew Brees, Major League Baseball's Clayton Kershaw, and the aforementioned Scottie Scheffler. Christianity has always been under attack, but in these tumultuous times—with mainstream media, Hollywood, and academia often using their own considerable platforms to denounce and even mock Christians and Christianity—it is more important than ever for those of faith with the megaphones their celebrity provides to use them to testify to their love of their Lord and Savior and to be heard above the secular din.

This is one front in a two-front war. The second front is that of declining attendance, not on Sunday afternoons in National Football League or Major League Baseball stadiums, but on Sunday mornings in churches. The secular din is getting louder, its choir expanding, and the news is disturbing. Pew Research Center reported in 2021 that those identifying themselves as Christians "make up 63% of the adult population." In September of 2022, the Pew Research Center published a story headlined: "Modeling the Future of Religion in America: If recent trends in religious switching continue, Christians could make up less than half of the U.S. population within a few decades."

Previously, the Pew Research Center had written: "The changes underway in the American religious landscape are broad-based. . . The Christian share of the population is down and religious 'nones' have grown across multiple demographic groups: white people, black people and Hispanics; men and women; in all regions of the country; and among college graduates and those with lower levels of educational attainment. Religious 'nones' are growing faster among Democrats than Republicans, though their ranks are swelling in both partisan coalitions. And although the religiously unaffiliated are on the rise among younger people and most groups of older adults, their growth is most pronounced among young adults."

In December of 2019, the American Enterprise Institute, a public policy think tank dedicated to promoting free people, free markets, and limited government, released a report titled "The decline of religion in American family life." Among its findings: "Approximately one in five (19 percent) Americans raised in a religious tradition no longer identify with any religion as an adult. But patterns of religious disaffiliation are not constant across demographic and political identities. Younger Americans report much greater rates of disaffiliation than do older Americans. Three in 10 (30 percent) young adults raised in a religious tradition growing up say they no longer affiliate with one as an adult. Among seniors, only 11 percent of those raised in a religion are currently unaffiliated."

The reasons are varied, but those who have an opportunity to help counter the decline and choose to remain silent won't help. What will help is responding the way Seattle Seahawks quarterback Russell Wilson did when he signed a new contract in 2019.

"My Hallelujah belongs to YOU. #AllForYourGlory," Wilson tweeted. A simple declaration from an athlete with a following in the millions can at least begin to help counter the stigma that Christianity is passé, uncool or, most disturbingly, unnecessary.

Curry and Wilson seem to understand this as they live their faith on and off the court and the field, subtly at times, but expansively when asked about it. Theirs is a standard to which Christian athletes, and Christians in general, should aspire. It isn't necessary to erect a big tent and hold a revival. Colloquies don't work in post-game interviews, but simple, unscripted, meaningful, and heart-felt professions of faith do.

Whatever it takes to advance the runners, to move the ball downfield, to put points on the board, as sportswriters and broadcasters say *ad nauseum*, though in this case the stakes are higher. The stakes are leading others to Christ.

Of course, many would prefer a separation of church and sports. Or church and everything else, for that matter. And given the hostility much of the culture and the mainstream media have for Christianity, it needs its vocal and visible advocates. Acquiescence should never be an option. Christian athletes who courageously defy the persecutors are to be encouraged, applauded, *prayed for*. The more of them there are, the more they can be heard above the secular din, enabling them to become beacons of faith and hope, to do as God commands in the Great Commission.

Sports as a forum for espousing Christianity and one's faith has been maligned throughout history, but it has persevered, in accordance with Luke's words: "But the seed on good soil stands for those with a noble and good heart, who hear the word, retain it, and by persevering produce a crop" (Luke 8:15 NIV).

But how did this union of faith and sports begin, where is it going, and what are the issues involved? It starts with the Bible, which, it should be noted, mentions sports and competition. For instance, the apostle Paul wrote, "Do you not know that in a race all the runners run, but only one gets the prize? Run in such a way as to get the prize. Everyone who competes in the games goes into strict training. They do it to get a crown that will not last, but we do it to get a crown that will last forever. Therefore I do not run like someone running aimlessly; I do not fight like a boxer beating the air. No, I strike a blow to my body and make it my slave so that after I have preached to others, I myself will not be disqualified for the prize" (1 Corinthians 9:24–27 NIV).

Paul also used a race as a metaphor for what had become his mission in life. He said to the Ephesian elders, "I consider my life worth nothing to me; my only aim is to finish the race and complete the task the Lord Jesus has given me—the task of testifying to the good news of God's grace" (Acts 20:24 NIV). And nearing the end of his life, he wrote in his often-recited letter to Timothy, "I have fought the good fight, I have finished the race, I have kept the faith" (2 Timothy 4:7 NIV).

Did you ever ponder whether God cares who wins, whether he picks winners? Or what roles Christian athletes on every level, from youth sports to professional sports, can play in this era of social media and expanded television coverage, in embracing the Great Commission?

The late Gary Carter, a Hall of Fame catcher with the Montreal Expos and New York Mets, among others, was exemplary in living out his faith in public. He was unafraid to use his platform to share the good news that is at the heart of Christianity, "that whoever believes in him shall not perish but have eternal life."

At his National Baseball Hall of Fame induction speech in Cooperstown, New York, in 2003, Carter said this: "I want to take this time to thank the most important people in my life. Above all, I want to thank my Lord and savior, Jesus Christ. A great verse that spoke to me while writing my speech, and kind of explains what it is all about, it comes in Psalm 18: 'I love you Lord, you are my strength. The Lord is my rock, my fortress, and my savior. And my God is my rock in whom I find protection. He is my shield, the strength of my salvation, and my stronghold. I will call on the Lord who is worthy of praise.' I praise the Lord, my God, my best friend, for giving me the ability, the desire, the love and the guidance that brought me here today. Without you, I would be nothing."

Those words, from a Christian's perspective, were the most

important of his twenty-plus minute speech, delivered to thousands on site and many more watching on television. And though we cannot know the impact those words had on listeners we can confidently say that the Holy Spirit used them effectively.

This is at the heart of the intersection of sports and Christianity, the power of one to change the world. One man or woman, with one speech, or one tweet—from the Gary Carters to the Tim Tebows and the Steph Currys—might help lead one person to Jesus, and they in turn might eventually bring others into the fold. And on and on. The Holy Spirit at work has no issue with running up the score in this regard.

As the late great evangelist Billy Graham said, "Courage is contagious. When a brave man takes a stand, the spines of others are often stiffened."

Christianity and sports have been uncomfortably inseparable for many in the media and maybe millions watching from home. But consider the dichotomy for those who prefer keeping them in their respective corners, á la church and state. It seems to escape them that Christian imagery is prevalent across the sports spectrum. We have the New Orleans Saints, the Hail Mary, the Holy Roller, the Immaculate Reception, the Padres, the Los Angeles Angels (which translates to "the Angels Angels"; I can't explain it, though more angels are better than fewer angels), Tommy Lasorda's Big Dodger in the Sky, Amen Corner at Augusta National, the Church Pew Bunkers at Oakmont Country Club, "God Bless America" sung at Philadelphia Flyers home games, Notre Dame's *Touchdown Jesus*, the mural of Jesus with arms raised on the side of the Hesburgh Library, overlooking the Fighting Irish's field.

Divorcing sports from Christianity is never going to happen, at least in a free society. The First Amendment of the Constitution of the United States of America guarantees it won't happen: "Congress shall make no law respecting an establishment of religion, or prohibiting the free exercise thereof. . ."

But the secular world no doubt will continue to throw up obstacles or to object vehemently, even attempting to shame Christian athletes into silence. The intersection of the two will remain open nonetheless, its traffic as busy as ever, collisions inevitable. So be it. One might argue that Christians always have the right of way by virtue of what intersections are.

They are, in fact, crossroads, emphasis on the cross.

TWO

Dusty Baker and the Power of Prayer

DUSTY BAKER IS an icon of leadership, his Hall of Fame-worthy résumé incontrovertibly the only evidence required. At seventy-three, he likely is the most widely respected man in Major League Baseball, one who in 2022 concluded his twenty-fifth season doing a job he never sought. Nearly twenty-two hundred managerial victories, twelve playoff teams, three Manager of the Year awards, three World Series teams, and a World Championship later, he revealed how it all began.

It all began with prayer.

Consulting a higher power might evoke quizzical looks from some in the fraternal order of baseball managers who never have considered there might be a greater authority than themselves. Those who challenge their decisions, or simply question them, I learned early in my twenty years of covering baseball, do so at their own risk. I once phrased a question, maybe poorly, to San Francisco Giants manager Frank Robinson that began with, "I assume . . ." His response, a condescending cliché, was this: "Never assume. When you assume, you make an *ass* out of *u* and *me*." Okay, then, thanks, Frank.

But Dusty Baker is different from most managers, by any metric.

I had come to know him when I was on the Dodgers beat for the *Orange County Register* from 1978 through 1980. He is accommodating, friendly, smart, with an infectious smile that perpetually exudes optimism. He too is entirely approachable, with one caveat. When a team is going poorly, reporters look to an intelligent go-to player to provide insight and perspective on the team's plight. Baker, in his playing career, harbored no patience for negativity, though he likely has to be more open as a manager.

I developed a great relationship with him, as did virtually anyone who had an opportunity to be around him on a daily basis, and to this day I regard him as one of the finest people I've been privileged to know in my long career in sports journalism. Those who don't appreciate him or respect him, I would argue, says more about them than it does about him.

Baker is the coolest manager, maybe the coolest man, in baseball, notwithstanding his age. He and his Dodgers teammate Glenn Burke were responsible for the first high five, a gesture that became ubiquitous in sports and in life after that. He still wears sweat bands, though he's not playing. And he still has fond memories of watching and hearing Jimi Hendrix play the guitar at the Monterey Pop Festival in 1967, "Woodstock before Woodstock," as *Sports Illustrated* called it, with tickets Baker's mother purchased for him for his high school graduation.

But he was different in another, more important way, a man who inherently understood the position espoused by the legendary UCLA basketball coach John Wooden. "There are many things that are essential to arriving at true peace of mind," Wooden said, "and one of the most important is faith, which cannot be acquired without prayer."

As the apostle Paul wrote, "Do not be anxious about anything, but in everything by prayer and supplication with thanksgiving let your requests be made known to God" (Philippians 4:6 ESV).

So here is Baker's faith story, culled from a long phone conversation I had with him post–World Series in 2021.

Baker's playing career had ended in 1986 after which he became a stockbroker. In April of 1987, *Nightline*'s Ted Koppel interviewed Dodgers General Manager Al Campanis before the fortieth anniversary of Jackie Robinson breaking baseball's color barrier. Campanis made disturbing remarks regarding the lack of minority representation in management positions, "that [African Americans] may not have some of the necessities to be, let's say, a field manager, or perhaps a general manager." Campanis, who incidentally roomed with Robinson in the minor leagues and revered him, was fired.

"It set off a recruiting blitz for minority managers and coaches," Baker said. "Me, Don Baylor, Cito Gaston, and Hal McRae." Coaching often is a dues-paying position for those with managerial aspirations. That was not Baker. "Last thing I wanted to do was coach," he said. "I did not want to coach."

Yet following the 1987 baseball season, San Francisco Giants general manager Al Rosen began courting him for a coaching position for the 1988 season. Baker listened, though apprehensively. First, he consulted with his earthly father. "I'm at a crossroads," he told his dad. "What should I do?"

"He said, 'go pray on it, son. Just go pray on it,'" Baker said. "So I went up to Lake Arrowhead [in the San Bernardino mountains in Southern California] to go pray on it. He used to tell me to go to the mountaintop or go to the water for serenity and clearness of mind. So I went to the mountaintop, in Lake Arrowhead, with my brother Vic and our daughters. And I was in line to check into our hotel there and somebody taps me on the shoulder, and it's Bob Lurie. I swear. The owner of the Giants. And he goes, 'Dusty, you need to come join us.'

"So I got on the phone to my dad and asked him, 'You think that was a sign?' He said, 'Son, you went up there to pray for answers, and before you checked into the hotel the sign tapped you on the shoulder.'"

When you talk to God, does he answer you? Dusty Baker would answer yes.

A Christian life begins with prayer, or as Martin Luther put it, "To be a Christian without prayer is no more possible than to be alive without breathing." Prayer is central to Baker's life and has been throughout. This might come as a surprise to many, though it shouldn't. Baker is open about his Christian faith, but that part of his biography amid his expanding popularity mostly goes unmentioned, unfortunately. He often has Christian books on his office desk. His testimony is available to anyone who asks. I asked.

Baker has spent his life navigating the intersection of Christianity and sports and has steadfastly leaned on his faith and his prayerful interactions with the Lord to guide him and his decisions, not all of which have been noble, as he readily admits. He is a sinner, as we all are, of course. "I don't always do what I'm supposed to do," he said. "But I know what I'm supposed to do. And you can ask forgiveness."

So he prays and does so, well, religiously, embracing the fact that a Christian life begins with prayer, and he unabashedly will talk about his faith and how prayer is the thread that stitches it to the forefront of his life.

I had been aware that Baker was a Christian and I was interested in speaking to him about his faith. I waited about a month after the conclusion of the 2021 World Series that the Astros lost in five games to the Atlanta Braves, the second time in his managerial career he had taken a team to the World Series. I had an old cell phone number that I wasn't sure was still good, so first I sent a text rather than cold-calling him. I was not even sure he'd remember me, thirty-two years after I had last spent time with him in 1989. I had been dispatched to San Francisco that summer to do a story on the Giants' Kevin Mitchell in advance of the All-Star Game in Anaheim. Mitchell was the best player in the National League that year, and Baker was a coach with the Giants, so my first stop in the Giants' clubhouse was to Dusty's locker to say hi. When he asked what I was doing there, I explained I was there to do a Mitchell story. Baker, as he has with so many other players, was mentoring Mitchell, an exceedingly talented player with issues, including a troubled past. "One time, we had a chapel speaker from San Quentin," Baker told me. "Three or four guys in there said to say hello to Kevin. They'd grown up together." So I wasn't sure what to expect from Mitchell, but Baker, without my asking, walked me over to Mitchell's locker, introduced us, and said to him that I was a friend and a good guy and that I was there to interview him. The interview was fantastic, and my respect for Baker grew, as did my appreciation for Mitchell.

Again, when I sent the text to Dusty in 2021, explaining that I wanted to speak to him about his faith, I wasn't sure how he would respond. But he replied within a day and said he'd call the following week.

Baker was raised a Baptist in Riverside, California, "against my will a lot of times," he said. "I went to Sunday school, then went to the sermon, then Baptist Training Union at night on Sundays. Our whole day was spent in the church. 'Train a child in the way he should go.' That was my case." He was citing Proverbs 22:6 (NKJV): "Train a child up in the way he should go, and when he is old he will not depart from it."

"They made me in charge of junior Sunday school, because I could memorize verses and was fairly smart in school. It was just something that carried me through my life, even though I wanted to be the thug. All the thugs were having fun in all the gangster movies. All the heroes were Billy the Kid and Jesse James on up to Cagney, Edgar G. Robinson, Baby Face Nelson. All the gangsters were the exciting guys. They always had a lot of money, pretty clothes, a lot of girls. My mom said, 'No son of mine is going to be a thug.'"

The family eventually moved to Sacramento, where he and his brother were the only African Americans in their high school. "It was a good thing I could play football and all the stuff that they stereotypically thought black kids could do," he said. "Then my junior year they discovered I had a heart murmur and made me skip football for five weeks, under supervision. I went back to the doctor, who told me I'd never play sports again. I was fifteen. All I wanted to do is be a professional. Not a professional baseball player. It was basketball first, then football, and then baseball. My heroes were Gale Sayers, Jim Brown, Elgin Baylor, and Tommy Davis.

"I prayed on it, 'Lord, please, no.' My dad then took me to a specialist in Oakland. I was praying like a dog on the way there, and when I got there, the doctor said there was nothing wrong with me, that I was a growing boy and I was going to grow out of that heart murmur I had."

During his senior year, Baker was conflicted, unsure of which sport to pursue following his high school graduation, though baseball prevailed. The night before the baseball draft in 1967, Baker prayed "that whatever team drafts me just don't let it be the Atlanta Braves, because I didn't want to go to the South," he said. "It was tough. There was a lot of racial unrest and anti-conformity all over the country, anti-Vietnam, anti-everything. This was sixty-seven, man, this was in the heat of everything."

Anti-Vietnam war protests and race riots dominated headlines in 1967. *U.S. News & World Report*, in its August 14, 1967, edition, wrote: "More than 100 cities of the U.S. have been hit by Negro violence this year. At least 177 persons have been killed, thousands injured. Property damage has approached 1 billion dollars."

On June 17, 1967, four days before the Major League Baseball draft, a race riot had begun in Atlanta, the beginning of a series of race riots that became known as the Long Hot Summer. The Atlanta riot lasted three days and did not go unnoticed by the nervous eighteen-year-old African American from Sacramento.

So he prayed. He prayed that a team from the South, of which there was one, the Braves, not draft him. "Then the Braves drafted me," Baker said.

"My dad didn't want me to sign. We went away for the weekend, to Dodger Stadium, and I signed with the Braves without my dad's permission. But I prayed on it the night before. That's what I tell people now. I tell my son, I tell everybody, you got a decision, you pray on it," he said fifty-four years later. "It might not be the decision that you want. Don't pray on it if you don't want a decision.

"So I signed with the Braves. I came home after two weeks with the Braves, then went to court with my mom and our lawyer against my dad and his lawyer. He tried to nullify my contract and he couldn't. They invoked the Jackie Coogan Law."

The law, named for a renowned child actor in the early twentieth century, was established to protect child performers' income. "So they put my money in a trust. In three years my money tripled. That's when I started watching the stock market. They put it in IBM stock and Standard Oil in California, which is now Chevron. I didn't talk to my dad for three years.

"So I had signed with the Braves. The best thing that happened to me was going to the South, and meeting Hank Aaron, and Andrew Young, and Jesse Jackson, and Ralph Abernathy, and all the civic leaders of that time through Hank Aaron. I'm telling you, every time when I don't pray on it, don't pray for an answer, it usually ends up screwed up. If I do pray on it, I may not get the answer that I want, but that's the answer that's best for me."

As the Dutch World War II hero and Christian icon Corrie ten Boom said, "Never be afraid to trust an unknown future to a known God."

Baker came to understand this, and prayer continued to serve as a compass in his life. When Aaron, his friend and mentor, was traded by Atlanta to the Milwaukee Brewers after the 1974 season, Baker prayed that he might return to the West Coast, and he was traded to the Los Angeles Dodgers a year later. He eventually ended his playing career in the Bay Area, one season with the Giants and two with the Oakland A's.

In 1988, guided by prayer, Baker accepted the Giants' offer to coach and gave himself five years to become a manager, either with the Giants or another team. "Five years and a day from the time I accepted the Giants [coaching] job, I was named the manager of the Giants, in 1993."

He has now managed five different teams—the Giants, the Chicago Cubs, the Cincinnati Reds, the Washington Nationals, and now the Houston Astros—and has taken two of them to the World Series, the Giants once and the Astros twice, and all five of them to the playoffs.

It is the nature of the managing profession that job security is nonexistent, and Baker has been fired four times. After the Reds fired him following the 2013 season in which they won ninety games, he had not intended to manage again.

He became a businessman, opening a winery in northern California, Baker Family Wines, and starting the Baker Energy Team that provides energy solutions to businesses and homes. Then the Washington Nationals called. Yet another crossroads.

"I had just started my business. I was torn between, do I leave what I was starting with my business and go back to baseball? Or how do I do it? The first person that I called was Joe Gibbs. I didn't even know Joe Gibbs, but I had admired him and had heard him speak on television."

Baker was aware that Gibbs had coached the Washington Redskins to three Super Bowl championships but had left coaching after the 1992 season to start Joe Gibbs Racing, a NASCAR team. He later returned to coaching.

"Somebody put me in contact with him and I was asking him some questions. 'How are you doing this and that?' And he told me that some in his family and other reputable people took over [his business while he was coaching], and at the end of the conversation he says, 'Let me pray with you, son.' This is my first meeting with him. He prays with me. I've got a lot of respect for Joe Gibbs. He didn't have to talk to me and he didn't have to pray with me and he didn't have to call me back."

Baker managed the Nationals for two years and they won ninety-five and ninety-seven games and finished first in the National League East both years. Then he was fired again, this three-time National League Manager of the Year. Odd business, baseball.

His age was now a factor, and the likelihood of his ever managing again was remote. Then came one more call. In January of 2020, Baker, at seventy-one, was hired to manage the Astros, who were in the throes of a cheating scandal dating to their World Series championship in 2017, but not exposed until late in 2019. They immediately became the most hated team in baseball. Their manager A. J. Hinch was implicated in the scandal and was fired following the 2019 season.

"I believe they didn't choose me [to manage the Astros], the Lord chose me," Baker said. "There's no way that I thought that they would even change managers. I prayed on it. I said, 'Lord, should I take this job?' Because it was a hard job. I've never been bombarded by this many negatives on a daily basis in my life."

The sports media rendered a verdict, that Baker was the right man at the right time to step into the most difficult managerial job in baseball. In late September of 2021, *Texas Monthly*'s Richard Justice expertly expressed what was a consensus opinion:

> "Baker seemed the perfect fit, given the respect he commands from players, for a position that required navigating the mine-field that the Astros' cheating scandal had created. Twenty months ago, the Houston Astros, knee-deep in scandal, could not have made a more perfect hire than Dusty Baker. Into the chaos swirling around Major League Baseball's most despised team stepped one of the game's great gentlemen and most successful managers."

When Jim Crane, the owner of the Astros, hired Baker, he had echoed this sentiment, though without acknowledging the minefield to which Justice alluded. "Throughout his successful career, Dusty has embodied the qualities that we were looking for in a manager," Crane said. "He's a winner, and more importantly, a strong leader who has earned the respect of not only his players, but of virtually everyone that he has touched in baseball. We're extremely excited to name Dusty as the new leader of our ballclub."

Baker took the Astros to the World Series in 2021 (they lost to the Atlanta Braves in six games), and then, at the age of seventy-two, in 2022, Baker was retained for a third season as manager of the Astros, who would win 104 games and return to and win the World Series.

He now ranks ninth on the list of most wins by managers, and all eight ahead of him are in the National Baseball Hall of Fame. His Astros winning the World Series in 2022, the capstone of his remark-able managerial career, in concert with a long playing career that included nearly 2,000 hits, 242 home runs, a Gold Glove for fielding excellence, that is certain to land him in the National Baseball Hall of Fame in Cooperstown, New York.

Baker, incidentally, called his opportunity to manage again, this time in Houston, a gift from God.

"It was already written," he said. "Some things are written. I believe the Lord might have kept me out here. It seems like I've had more influence on young people in society during this year-and-a-half tenure than I had the whole time before. This is a tough time in our country, a tough time racially, politically, economically, the pandemic. I never experienced more people that were mad and more hatred than I have during these periods. Every day there's a damn shooting at a school. Or people drive a car into a parade of kids. What's going on, man? You know what I mean? I think it's the devil. The devil, hoo boy, he's running wild, brother. You tell people that and they're, 'Ah, nah, nah.' Okay, man.

"One of the greatest things in my life right now is, I'm a grandfather. I have a forty-two-year-old daughter [Natosha] and then my son [Darren], twenty-two. When he's home, he comes in and we say our prayers every night before he goes to bed. That's one of the greatest things, to see my daughter, who's Christian, and my grandson, and to see my son. I tell my son, 'You can't be afraid of backlash. There are quite a few people who are believers and quite a few nonbelievers who are going to chastise you for believing. You've got to stand up for what you believe.'"

Darren Baker, incidentally, played baseball at the University of California Berkeley, was a tenth-round draft pick of the Washington Nationals, and now is playing in their farm system.

Those looking for a powerful testimony of Christian faith and of the importance, indeed, the necessity, of prayer, need not look further than the example of Dusty Baker.

THREE

The Tebow Template

THE SIDEBAR on East 15th Street in New York City billed itself as "NYC's Best Sports Bar in Union Square," and maybe it was, though attempting to quantify its claim likely would have required a turnstile count on a Sunday during football season. Or a keg count. Either way, it did not fit what might be a traditional definition of a sports bar. It was more upscale than lowbrow, more diva than dive, a bar that until it went out of business during the COVID-19 pandemic catered to young urban professionals who wouldn't necessarily recoil at the sight of kale Caesar salad or truffle mushroom flatbread on their menus.

On the upside, for those who judge sports bars on, well, sports, it had twenty-one high-definition televisions, all of them on fall Sundays tuned to various National Football League games being played around the country. They attracted Giants and Jets fans, obviously, but also all manner of New York City transplants who staked out a barstool or a table from which to watch their hometown teams play games that might not have been televised nationally. Supporting sideBAR's claim to be the best sports bar in Union Square was that many of those fans were rabid.

Among the rabid congregating at sideBAR on October 23, 2011,

was Colorado native Jared Kleinstein, a diehard Broncos fan, who
had come to New York City to work for StreetEasy, a real estate
concern there. He was joined at the bar by his crew of five. They
were there to watch the pitiful play the hapless, the Broncos versus
the Miami Dolphins, at Sun Life Stadium (now Hard Rock Stadium)
in South Florida. This was no Super Bowl prelude. More likely, it
was a matchup of teams vying for the worst record in the NFL and
the first pick in the draft the following April. The Broncos' record
was 1-4, the Dolphins' 0-5.

The week prior, Denver coach John Fox had benched struggling
quarterback Kyle Orton at halftime, replacing him with Tim Tebow,
the Broncos' heralded first-round draft choice the year before. Tebow
had won the Heisman Trophy as a University of Florida sophomore
in 2007 and was a finalist for the Heisman in 2008 and 2009. He had
been the twenty-fifth player chosen in the first round of the NFL
draft in 2010, yet despite his remarkable college credentials he
largely was an athletic enigma.

Tebow delivered a measure of excitement to the moribund
Broncos in the second half, running for a touchdown and passing for
another, though Denver still lost. But Tebow had played well enough
to earn a start against the Dolphins, heightening anticipation among
Broncos fans, both in Colorado and across the nation, as well as
Florida Gators fans and others eagerly waiting to see whether
Tebow's college prowess could transfer to the professional game.
Tebow mania had not yet reached a fever pitch, but the intrigue was
growing.

For most of the game with Miami, it was more of the same for
the Broncos, who were on the verge of a fifth loss in six games. They
were trailing, 15-0, with a little more than five minutes remaining—
virtually a hopeless cause, more so with Tebow, for whom moving
the ball downfield had been an uphill climb to that point. It brought
to mind the old saying, *on a wing and a prayer*. At that point, the
Broncos had a far better chance with a prayer than with Tebow's
wing. Their previous seven possessions had resulted in six punts and
one lost fumble. Kleinstein and friends hung around anyway.

Suddenly, Tebow began throwing and running in a manner that recalled his glory days at Florida, and no doubt many—possibly including unbelievers, too—considered the possibility that divine intervention was at play. In the final two and a half minutes Tebow threw two touchdown passes, the latter with seventeen seconds left in the game. He then ran for a two-point conversion to tie the score, sending the game into overtime. Denver eventually won on a field goal, a remarkable comeback victory for a team destined to go nowhere other than home later that day.

Tebow, an outspoken Christian, born in the Philippines of Baptist missionaries from Florida, had been kneeling on one knee, head bowed, and saying a quick prayer before and after games—win, lose, or draw—going back to high school, when few noticed or cared. This time, though, cameras were homed in on him as he took a knee, bowed his head, and prayed, a private moment in a public arena transmitted via satellite to televisions around the country, including one at the sideBAR a few blocks from Union Square, in the East Village of America's largest city.

In the euphoria of the Broncos' improbable victory, Kleinstein had an idea. "When we were celebrating," he said when I spoke with him several years later, "I said, 'let's take a picture doing a Tebow. Let's replicate that.'"

Kleinstein and friends walked outside the sideBAR, lined up, kneeled, and struck a Tebow pose while another bar patron took a photo of them doing so. Kleinstein posted the photo on Facebook that night and called it Tebowing. "And it got nine likes," he said. "I said to myself, 'That's viral,' which was pretty hilarious to think back then. Then I bought the URL tebowing.com. Designed it that night and sent it to my friends late Sunday night, and said let's do this as the new planking. The friends I sent it to shared it with their friends who shared it with their friends who shared it with their friends. It went from there.

"Monday I made a joke to my boss, and I said by the end of the week I'm going to have more people using this than StreetEasy, and we were like the number one real estate website in New York. He said, 'OK, I'm going to take that bet.' Wednesday morning in the office, I turned on the TV and CNN was talking about it. That's when I knew it was crazy. By Friday we had more unique users [than StreetEasy]. I was like, oh my God, I actually won the bet."

Five days after the game, Lindsay H. Jones of the *Denver Post* followed up with a report on Tebow mania:

"What's funny about it is how rapidly it's caught on, and how much it has taken off," Tebow said Friday in the Broncos' locker room.

Tebow said he understands that some people might be using Tebowing to mock him, or religion in general. He is more excited, though, about those who are taking it seriously.

"It's not my job to see peoples' reasons behind it, but I know (of a kid) with cancer that tweeted me, 'Tebowing while I'm chemoing' — how cool is that?" Tebow said. "That's worth it right now. If that gives him any encouragement or puts a smile on his face, or gives him encouragement to pray, that's completely awesome."

Eventually, 22.5 million people went to the tebowing.com website, Kleinstein said, with nearly twenty-three million page views. Tebowing was featured on the television show *South Park*, while a couple of episodes of Tim Allen's sitcom *Last Man Standing*, set in Denver, featured characters Tebowing. "It was an amazing time," Kleinstein said. "My dad passed about two-and-a-half years ago. I looked through his old files and he had a whole file of Tebowing media newsclips. That was one of my favorite things."

Kleinstein throughout was careful to communicate that he "wasn't trying to offend anybody, that people understood it was never making fun of Tim, it was supporting him and trying to honor him.

"If we all would be a little bit reflective—people describe it as genuflecting—if more people had that kind of experience because of the Tebowing meme, something that's kind of a fun, playful thing, can lead to a bit more introspection on genuflecting, then the world may be a little bit of a better place."

The kicker to this episode is that Kleinstein is Jewish. Yet he readily understood and acknowledged the positive impact that this Christian man kneeling in prayer, seen by millions, could have had.

It was a simple gesture by a renowned athlete wholly unafraid to live out his Christian faith in a public arena, indifferent to offending, and his "Tebowing" impacted—at a minimum, though the number likely was substantially higher—a single life, the child with cancer who was "Tebowing while chemo-ing." That alone qualifies it as a success, and a worthwhile gesture in accordance with the Bible: "Each of you should use whatever gift you have received to serve others, as faithful stewards of God's grace in its various forms. If anyone speaks, they should do so as one who speaks the very words of God. If anyone serves, they should do so with the strength God provides, so that in all things God may be praised through Jesus Christ. To him be the glory and the power forever and ever. Amen" (1 Peter 4:10–11 NIV).

Tim Tebow largely has lived his adult life in what the legendary sportswriter Dan Jenkins called "the big window." Television. The medium is unsparing in revealing flaws, be they in performance or personal behavior. Tebow was a legendary college football player who had a short-lived NFL career and a forgettable minor league baseball career. But he has lived an exemplary life in public from the moment he set foot on the University of Florida campus in Gainesville, Florida.

Fame is a powerful conduit for the Christian witness, as Tebow learned early in life. In 2008, then a junior at the University of Florida, he saw teammates putting eye-black patches beneath their eyes, ostensibly as a means of reducing glare (others can argue the efficacy of doing so; I am not convinced). He noticed that some were "putting their mom's name or their area code" on the black patches.

"I started to think, you know, I wonder if I could put on eye black, grab a silver sharpie and put something on there that could be encouraging or inspiring or uplift somebody."

The thought occurred to him that he could reference a Bible verse on there. He came up with Philippians 4:13, "I can do all things through Christ who strengthens me," he said, reciting the verse. "That's an awesome verse for a football player."

It attracted some notice, but he kept doing it every week, writing "Phil" on the black patch under his right eye and "4:13" on the patch under his left eye, and it began attracting greater attention, notably among Florida Gator fans. Moments before the team was to exit its locker room for the start of its Southeastern Conference championship game with Alabama, "at this moment, I really felt like God was putting it on my heart to change the verse," he said. "I was like, 'Really? Right now?' But I kind of stepped back for a second and realized that if we won, we'd be playing in the national championship and that would be maybe the biggest stage that I would ever get to change the verse and put something meaningful on there."

Florida defeated Alabama and advanced to the national championship game, to be played six weeks later, on January 8, 2009. He began contemplating what verse to use. "God kept bringing to my heart and my head John 3:16," he said. "That's the essence of our Christianity, it's the essence of our hope."

So that was the verse he chose.

> *For God so loved the world, that he gave his only*
> *Son, that whoever believes in him should not*
> *perish but have eternal life. (John 3:16 ESV)*

When he informed his parents of his decision two nights before the game, his father asked, "Have you told Coach [Urban] Meyer?"

Good question, regarding a superstitious coach who was a stickler for routine. So the next day, he informed Coach Meyer of his decision. Meyer was incredulous.

"What are you talking about? You can't change the verse," Meyer said. "That verse got us here."

Tebow explained his reasoning and Meyer gave his consent. Florida went on to defeat Oklahoma, 24-14, to win the national championship. Two days later, he was with his family and Coach Meyer at Ballyhoo Grill in Gainesville, "eating grouper," he said, when the coach received a phone call.

"Mm. Uh huh. All right. Bye," Meyer said, according to Tebow's account in a bylined story on the *LifeWay Voices* website.

"I looked at him and I was like, 'What was that all about?' He told me who it was, our PR guy, and he said, 'Timmy, he just told me that during that game ninety-four million people Googled John 3:16.'

"And honestly, my first thought was, 'How the heck do ninety-four million people not know John 3:16? It's Sunday school, bro. That's the first thing you hear.'

"But it was just so humbling for me sitting in that restaurant, thinking about how big the God that we serve really is. Like, really, how big the God that we serve really is. So many times we put Him in a box. But no, the God that created us, the God that has a plan for us, the God that wrote a poem about your life, He is a big God that wants to do amazing things. And when we just turn around and say, 'Hey, here God,' it might not feel like a lot. Guess what? He can perform miracles. He can do amazing things. And I really believe the God that we worship wants to do amazing things in us and through us."

One man, albeit one with a high profile, and a simple gesture— one word, John, and three numerals, 3, 1, and 6—reached nearly 100 million people on Google alone. The crowd at Dolphin Stadium in Miami Gardens, Florida, was nearly 80,000. The Nielsen Ratings reported the game was viewed by nearly 27 million. Who knows how many others saw video or photos of Tebow with "John 3:16" on his eye black?

Whatever the number of those to whom Tebow witnessed in that game alone, it was staggering.

Tebow, meanwhile, continued to live out his faith in a very public manner, without concern for backlash, in accordance with what the Lord said to Paul: "And the Lord said to Paul one night in a vision,

'Do not be afraid, but go on speaking and do not be silent'" (Acts 18:9 ESV).

Super Bowl XLIV in January 2010 was a definitive example of his adherence to the scripture and steadfast reluctance to cave to public pressure. He and his mother Pamela agreed to do a pro-life Super Bowl commercial paid for by Focus on the Family, a Christian concern located in Colorado Springs and founded by Dr. James Dobson.

I should disclose that my wife Marlene, daughter Hannah, and I have a long and important history with Focus on the Family and Dr. Dobson, though he had left the organization in 2009. We remain close to Dr. Dobson and are still supportive of Focus on the Family.

The ad's theme was "Celebrate Family, Celebrate Life." When Pamela was pregnant with Tim and fell ill during a missionary trip in the Philippines, a doctor recommended that she have an abortion, that she "needed to abort quickly and my life was in danger," Pamela told *First Coast News* in Jacksonville, Florida. "She said I would die and he wasn't really a baby, he was a mass of fetal tissue.

"When [my doctor] delivered Timmy, he said it was the biggest miracle he had ever been a part of. He had never seen anything like it and he couldn't explain it. There was just a tiny piece of placenta that was attached to him and he said there was no explanation for how he survived all of those months in the womb."

The 30-second ad, at a cost of $2.5 million or more, was, as it intended to be, a celebration of life. That did not appease the ardent pro-choice faction of America, including those who had attempted to keep the ad from appearing. "An ad that uses sports to divide rather than to unite has no place in the biggest national sports event of the year—an event designed to bring Americans together," Jehmu Greene, president of the Women's Media Center in New York City, told *CBS News*. The Women's Media Center had support from the National Organization for Women and the Feminist Majority, CBS News reported.

Tebow, preparing for the Senior Bowl in Mobile, Alabama, addressed reporters there on the controversy. "I know some people won't agree with it, but I think they can at least respect that I stand up for what I believe," he said. "I've always been very convicted of it [his views on abortion] because that's the reason I'm here, because my mom was a very courageous woman. So any way that I could help, I would do it."

Twitter, meanwhile, was still relatively in its infancy in 2009. By September of 2011, a month before the advent of Tebowing, it had reached 100 million active monthly users and it would more than double in the next year.

The Broncos, in 2011, would lose the week after the Tebowing phenomenon began, but then won six straight games and eventually made the playoffs as a wild-card team. On January 8, 2012, three years to the day after Tebow's John 3:16 set Google atwitter, the Broncos, 8-8 on the regular season, played the Pittsburgh Steelers, 12-4, in the wild-card playoff game at Sports Authority Field in Denver.

This was a mismatch on paper, unless the paper was parchment— a Biblical joke, I confess. The betting line favored the Steelers, eight-point favorites. Yet the Broncos somehow played the Steelers even through sixty minutes, the score tied, 23-23, to send the game into overtime.

On the first play from scrimmage in overtime, from Denver's twenty-yard line, Tebow connected with wide receiver Demaryius Thomas on a pass across the middle and Thomas sprinted to a touch-down, an eighty-yard play that gave the Broncos an unlikely 29-23 victory.

One can only guess the number of Broncos fans Tebowing in the wake of this upset win. It would have been greater had they been aware at the time of the remarkable "coincidences" later revealed. Again, three years to the day after his John 3:16 eye-black phenomenon, he passed for 316 yards. He averaged 3.16 yards per carry. He averaged 31.6 yards per completion. The Broncos' time of possession was 31:06. The television rating was 31.6. And another ninety million people Googled John 3:16.

"And as I was just standing in that hallway thinking, 'God, I didn't know that you were doing anything.'. . . But it's amazing how big the God is that we serve. He took something that I did three-and-a-half years ago, to make a decision to put Philippians 4:13 and then change it for one game. But I thought, 'Hey, this is really cool. We impacted some people, but it's done.' But no, God has an awesome plan and you might not even see what He's doing. You might not even know how He's working. But the amazing thing is, when we step out and we show a little courage. . . a little boldness, what God can do with it in our lives, through our lives."

No kidding. The Billy Graham Evangelistic Association has a website, PeaceWithGod.net, and a ministry called Search for Jesus. "Taking advantage of John 3:16's popularity in Google searches on Monday," Trevor Freeze wrote on the website, "the [Billy Graham Evangelistic Association] advertised a PeaceWithGod.net landing page around searches for John 3:16. . . Over 7,000 users specifically inquiring about John 3:16 this week have landed on PeaceWith-God.net via Google, with more than 100 clicking they had made a decision to accept Jesus Christ into their life."

The higher the profile, the bigger the target, of course, and predictably Tebow absorbed his share of shots, cheap or otherwise. The former included Stephen Tulloch and Tony Scheffler of the Detroit Lions in a game with the Broncos, each of them Tebowing, Tulloch after sacking Tebow and Scheffler after catching a touchdown pass. On another Sunday, "Oakland Raiders' fans held signs that read 'Welcome to Hell,' directed at Tebow during the pre-game warm-ups before Sunday's NFL match-up in Oakland," the *Christian Post* reported.

Let me interject here that I was on the Los Angeles Raiders beat for a newspaper for one season twenty-five-some years earlier, and if that was the best insult their fans could conjure up in 2011, they clearly were working with a depleted supply of venom. Their fans were, to say as politely as possible, interesting.

Tebow, as he is predisposed to doing, always took the high road, saying simply that he hadn't seen the gestures and that he was not bothered by them.

In February of 2020, days after the Kansas City Chiefs had won the Super Bowl, Tebow was in Overland Park, Kansas, to give the keynote speech at Kansans for Life's annual Valentine's Day banquet.

"It really does mean a lot more than winning the Super Bowl," Tebow told the crowd. "One day, when you look back and people are talking about you and they say, 'Oh, my gosh, what are you going to be known for?' Are you going to say Super Bowl or we saved a lot of babies?"

Tebow has never wavered, however large and loud the chorus of opposition got, in using the platforms available to him to express his faith. He has been a veritable profile in courage for others to follow in adherence to God's command in the Great Commission.

FOUR

Peach Baskets to Rafer Johnson: The Influencers

"HISTORY," the renowned Christian author C. S. Lewis wrote, "is a story written by the finger of God." It was sports' good fortune, I submit, that that prolific finger belonging to the creator of all things, from whom all blessings flow, gave us James Naismith. Not because Naismith gave us basketball, but *why* he gave us basketball.

Long before social media, before iPhones, computers, television, telephones, even before homes were lit by electricity, sports were intersecting with Christianity, and our games were identified by some as a means to share the message of Christ. Yes, long before there was Tebowing. Or tweeting, too.

Naismith, a Canadian and a devout Christian intending to enter the ministry, played rugby and football at McGill University in Montreal. "It was while playing football at McGill that I received one of my strongest urges to make athletics become an avenue of preaching," Naismith wrote in the January 1939 edition of *The Rotarian*. "One day in practice something went wrong, and the guard next to me let loose a stream of profanity. Suddenly he stopped and exclaimed: 'Excuse me, Jim. I'm sorry.'"

This was the impetus behind Naismith's decision to forgo a career in formal preaching, "that I thought that there might be other effective ways of doing good besides preaching," he said. Still, he decided to enroll at Presbyterian College Theological Seminary in Montreal to earn a theology degree as a fallback position. He then moved to Springfield, Massachusetts, and enrolled in the International YMCA Training School to study physical education. On his application, he defined his goal that has been an enduring hallmark of his biography: To "win men for the Master."

It was at the Young Men's Christian Training School (now called Springfield College) that he met Amos Alonzo Stagg, who had gone to Yale and starred in football while pursuing a career in the ministry. Stagg's own career goals changed when he opted for teaching instead of preaching.

Dr. Luther Gulick, the Dean of the Physical Education Department at the Young Men's Christian Training School, aware of Stagg's football prowess, suggested that the time was right to start a football program at the school and that he wanted Stagg to coach it. Naismith was one of thirteen who made Stagg's team and was its center.

Stagg, though having abandoned his plans to join the ministry, still had a ministerial impact and was an early example of using sports as a platform for exposing others to Christianity. He offered up a simple prayer to his team before every game.

"Let us pray for God's blessing on our game," Stagg said.

"He did not pray for victory, but he prayed that each man should do his best and show the true Christian spirit," Naismith wrote in his book, *Basket Ball: Its Origin and Development*. He originally called his game basket ball, two words. "For two years it was [Stagg's] custom to ask different members of the team to lead; during those two years I never heard anything but the same spirit breathed by the men. Our team averaged less than one-hundred-sixty pounds, but we played games with Harvard, Yale, Amherst, and other large colleges. We won our share of the games, and our team became known as 'Stagg's Stubby Christians.'"

Dr. Gulick, meanwhile, was searching for a new indoor activity to engage students and assist with their physical fitness during the cold winter months. He assigned the task to Naismith. "His charge was to create a game that was easy to assimilate, yet complex enough to be interesting. It had to be playable indoors or on any kind of ground, and by a large number of players all at once," noted a story headlined "Basketball Was Born Here," published by Springfield College. "It should provide plenty of exercise, yet without the roughness of football, soccer, or rugby since those would threaten bruises and broken bones if played in a confined space."

Naismith devised a game that included a ball big enough that it could not be hidden. He had two peach baskets nailed to the lower rail of the gymnasium balcony encircling the floor, the rail precisely ten feet above the floor, as it were. He stationed a man by each peach basket to pluck the ball from them after a team scored to return it to play. Nice concept, but it took a while before anyone figured out that by cutting the bottoms out of the peach baskets men no longer would be required to retrieve the ball from the baskets, thus expediting play in the process. Notwithstanding the inconvenience of having to retrieve a ball stuck in a peach basket ten feet above the floor, the game of *basket ball* instantly became popular.

Decades later, Naismith pondered what he had created. "I am sure that no man can derive more satisfaction from money or power than I do from seeing a pair of basketball goals in some out-of-the-way place. Deep in the Wisconsin woods. . . high in the Colorado mountains. . . halfway across the desert—all are constant reminders that I have at least partially accomplished the objective that I set up."

Naismith died in 1939, at the age of seventy-eight. It is doubtful he would recognize his creation today, though he likely would be astonished by the skill with which it is played and by its worldwide popularity. Similarly, he likely would be disappointed that his original mission, *to win men for the Master*, is mostly forgotten, notwithstanding Golden State Warriors star Steph Curry unabashedly and frequently professing his Christian faith.

Fortunately, the baton has never been dropped altogether. Here is Chuck Colson writing for the *Christian Post* in 2011:

In the last 100 years, we've seen no shortage of Christian
athletes who use their skill, self-discipline, and sportsmanship
as a witness to Christ – from Olympic runner Eric Liddel in
the 1920s to football player Tim Tebow in our own
generation.

Liddel was the subject of an Academy Award-winning film,
Chariots of Fire. Known as the Flying Scotsman, he was the son of
Christian missionaries and later a missionary himself who won a
gold medal in the 400 meters in the 1924 Olympics in Paris. He was
a missionary preaching the Gospel in China during World War II and
was interned in a Japanese-run camp. He died there five months
before liberation in 1945.

The point is that Naismith, Stagg, and Liddel established a prece-
dent for using sports to promote Christianity. Today, the audiences
are enormous, providing athletes unafraid to espouse their Christian
faith with the potential to change lives, to win men and women, boy
and girl, for the Master.

It was a blueprint of sorts for generations of Christian athletes to
similarly use their skills and the platforms those skills presented
them to win men for the Master, as Tim Tebow has done from the
moment he entered college at Florida, and as the great decathlete
Rafer Johnson had done before him.

Johnson was the gold medalist in the decathlon in the 1960
Olympic Games in Rome after winning the silver medal in the same
event in 1956. He lit the Olympic cauldron at the Los Angeles
Memorial Coliseum to open the 1984 Olympics. His remarkable
biography included his role in the founding of the Special Olympics,
and he was an accomplished actor, too.

Johnson wrote this in 1962 for *Christian Athlete,* the flagship
publication of the Fellowship of Christian Athletes:

I've attended church ever since I can remember. I can thank
my mother and father for this, because they saw to it that
their children attended Sunday school and church regularly. I

was in the church choir, gave my offerings, and was, in general, very active in its program. But even with all my church activities, I was not sure that my life was lined up with God's will.

On October 29, 1953, I realized that I could never be lined up with His will until I accepted His Son Jesus Christ by faith as my personal Savior. There wasn't much emotion as I did this, but later, when I realized that He was blessing my commitment in many ways, the tears really flowed. I don't know when I've ever felt happier. Since then I have come to see how anyone can achieve victory in life through Jesus Christ. We experience this when we acknowledge that the achievement is all his. Through our faith, we share in His victory.

Depending upon Him this way, I found that I could face problems without fear and discouragement. No matter how big or small the problem, He was always present and ready to help. Philippians 4:13 is certainly true: "I can do all things in him who strengthens me" (RSV). . .

I come to each athletic event conditioned physically and mentally. But spiritual conditioning is the most important of all. This means I am prepared to run each race, compete in each contest, not for my glory but for the glory of my Lord.

Ever since I became a Christian in my junior year of high school, I have loved Jesus Christ with all my heart. He is the leader of my life and without Him I would be lost for He is all.

Johnson was blessed with amazing skills in a variety of fields, but he never failed to credit our Lord and Savior. He set a standard for the Christian athlete.

I spoke with former Dodgers radio broadcaster Ross Porter about

Rafer Johnson, with whom he worked at KNBC television in Los Angeles in 1966 and developed an enduring friendship. Both Porter and Johnson were sports reporters on the nightly news broadcasts, with Tom Brokaw anchoring. I knew Ross from my days on the Dodgers beat. For twenty-eight seasons, Porter was a Dodgers' radio broadcaster working alongside Vin Scully, another Christian man who was unafraid to talk about his faith.

"When I started with Rafer I knew all about his spirituality," Porter said. "It turned out my family ended up going to the same church as he did, Bel Air Presbyterian. Donn Moomaw was the pastor." Moomaw had been a star on UCLA's undefeated football team in 1954, yet turned down an opportunity to play in the NFL to pursue a career in the ministry. "Our oldest daughter Rosalyn was teaching second graders in Sunday school at Bel Air Presbyterian and Rafer joined her. He was there every Sunday with her. His whole idea was, 'I'm here for one reason. I want to be some sort of guide, to help the young boys just getting started who needed to know about God.'

"My wife Lin asked him one time, 'Rafer, looking at your life and what you had going, you could have been anything you wanted to be, a TV star, a movie star.' He said, 'Lin, all I wanted to do is to give back because of the people who helped me along the way.' His whole life was helping others and giving back. His whole life was a religious service to people."

Porter recalled the night that Rafer Johnson's dear friend Robert F. Kennedy, a presidential candidate, was assassinated in June of 1968 at the Ambassador Hotel in Los Angeles. Johnson was by his side when Sirhan Sirhan pulled out a gun and killed Kennedy. Johnson was among those wrestling Sirhan to the ground, and Rafer wound up taking the gun from him.

"He later told us after all the Secret Service people questioned him at the hotel that he went home like at four o'clock in the morning," Porter said, "and as he was undressing he reached in his coat pocket and there was the gun that Sirhan had used. He said, 'I called the officer and said I think I have something you'd like to have.'

"He was doing the eleven o'clock sports on Channel 4 [KNBC] at the time. Bobby Kennedy and he were like brothers. When Bobby was assassinated, he never went back to Channel 4, he was so torn up. He told us he would sit in his living room with the blinds closed, and just sit there, so depressed. Then one day his wife brought him the phone and said, 'Here's a phone call you ought to take.' The voice on the other end said, 'Rafer, this is Eunice [Shriver, Bobby Kennedy's sister]. I know that you're in despair like the rest of us. But if Bobby were here today, he'd tell you you've got to get up and do something to help, and I'm calling you to help me start Special Olympics.'"

The servant's heart prevailed over the mourner in despair. Rafer Johnson was one of the original board members recruited by Eunice Shriver. "He told us that the first day he went to a Special Olympics get-together there were fifteen youngsters there," Porter said. "At the time he finally bowed out of doing it there were 30,000 youngsters participating in Special Olympics.

"That's what he wanted to do. He just wanted to help. Lin had a good definition of him. She said that his faith was the core strength of his life. All he did was for good. Giving back was so important to him. I asked him several times about that. He said, 'I just want to help other people.'"

Rafer Johnson was of the lineage of prominent sports personalities that began with Amos Alonzo Stagg. These individuals used their prestige and Christian faith to set a standard of service to others, spreading the word of God in the process, while providing a blueprint for Christians of all stripes to follow. For Christian athletes, it's an example of not promoting themselves, but promoting the path to everlasting life according to John 3:16.

"Rafer Johnson," Porter said emphatically, "is one of the finest people I've ever known."

FIVE

The Elysian Fields

BASEBALL no longer is the most popular sport in America, the game having ceded to football its standing once exemplified in the old saw *as American as apple pie*. Yet an argument could be made that baseball remains the most beloved—the summer game, as it is affectionately called, its sparkling diamonds still trumping gridirons. The game remains evocative of times past—simpler times, of warm summer nights, hot dogs, Sunday doubleheaders, peanuts and Cracker Jack, and fathers having a catch with sons, now happily having been expanded to fathers or mothers having a catch with sons or daughters.

"I don't have to tell you that the one constant through all the years has been baseball," author W.P. Kinsella wrote in his novel *Shoeless Joe*, the basis for the popular film *Field of Dreams*. "America has been erased like a blackboard, only to be rebuilt and then erased again. But baseball has marked time while America has rolled by like a procession of steamrollers."

Over the years, the game has been romanticized in poetry, in film, even in music, the latter in "Talkin' Baseball" by Terry Cashman, also known as the Willie, Mickey, and the Duke song. Its original sheet music is in the National Baseball Hall of Fame in Cooperstown, N.Y.

The erudite *Washington Post* columnist George Will, unapologetically a rabid baseball fan, wrote, "Baseball is a habit. The slowly rising crescendo of each game, the rhythm of the long season—these are the essentials and they are remarkably unchanged over nearly a century and a half. Of how many American institutions can that be said?" Another renowned *Washington Post* columnist, a legend and an avid baseball fan, was the great Charles Krauthammer, who wrote this about his favorite pastime: "Baseball is a slow, boring, complex, cerebral game that doesn't lend itself to histrionics. You 'take in' a baseball game, something odd to say about a football or basketball game, with the clock running and the bodies flying."

The film *Field of Dreams* entertainingly and emotionally captured America's love affair with baseball, including a father and son "having a catch."

My own earliest memory of the game is of playing catch with my dad on the sidewalk in front of our house on East 68th Street (now NE 68th Street) across from Roosevelt High School in Seattle. I was the pitcher, he was the catcher, and I peppered him with my slow, high-arching *fastball,* provided it did not bounce first.

I too recall watching a Little League game in the neighborhood, longing to be a part of it, to wear a uniform, to join a team, to participate, win or lose, in the traditional post-game salute to the opposing team that I still vividly remember decades later: "Two bits, four bits, six bits a dollar, all for Hasty Tasty stand up and holler."

My own life-long love affair with the game began with those memories, starting with a catch with my father.

Reverence for baseball often takes on a religious aura among the faithful, and, like any actual religion, in this case Christianity, there is the good, the bad, and the ugly, with comic relief occasionally intervening. Sacrilege, too.

Dodger Stadium, the home of the Los Angeles Dodgers since 1962, is an edifice its late Hall of Fame manager Tommy Lasorda called "blue heaven on earth." He often said, "If you want to get to heaven, you gotta go through Dodger Stadium." The stadium, in fact, was constructed on a plot of land called Elysian Park Heights —*Elysian*, from Greek mythology, suggesting paradise or heavenly. Elysian Park Heights is situated a few blocks north of downtown Los Angeles, in Chavez Ravine.

Yet it is not heaven, blue or otherwise, given the less than honorable way it came to be home to the Dodgers. The stadium was built on land that had been home to many Mexican American families who were forced to sell their houses below market value. The land was seized via eminent domain, as a means of providing incentive, via a proposed stadium site, for the Brooklyn Dodgers to move west. The *Los Angeles Times* noted that on May 8, 1959, "The remaining residents of the Chavez Ravine community are forcibly evicted from their homes to allow construction on the stadium to begin. Police were called after residents refused to leave. The fray lasted about two hours. After the eviction, bulldozers leveled structures on the property."

The property seizure has been a footnote largely ignored or forgotten in the history of the stadium, except perhaps to those families whose lives were ignominiously upended. Lasorda nonetheless was the greatest ambassador for the stadium, *blue heaven on earth,* and its tenants, the Dodgers, and maybe of the game of baseball itself.

But, as beautiful as it is and how much I enjoyed going there, it is not heaven on earth, and to suggest otherwise borders on blasphemy.

Lasorda was given to hyperbole, of course, contributing to his reputation as one of baseball's greatest characters, albeit a cartoon character at times. He often had run-ins with team mascots, foremost among them the Phillie Phanatic (Philadelphia Phillies), Youppi (Montreal Expos), and the San Diego Chicken (Padres), who he once threatened to strangle.

He also was legendarily profane to a degree, as the saying goes, that would make a longshoreman blush, and occasionally leaving the impression his vocabulary contained few words that exceeded four letters. His language was often so blue his Dodgers' cap looked bleached by comparison. Most famous among his blue tirades came in the wake of the Giants' Dave Kingman hitting three home runs in a game against the Dodgers. A radio reporter asked Lasorda for his opinion of Kingman's performance. His memorable and often replayed response is not family friendly.

I ran afoul of Lasorda early in my tenure covering the Dodgers, and on more than one occasion was on the receiving end of his expletive-laced vitriol. No saint myself, I occasionally let my personal opinions of him unnecessarily influence my writing, triggering further confrontations and tirades, the latter usually one-sided. The first time came in the summer of 1979, when heading into the All-Star break, the two-time defending National League champions were foundering. I wrote a story, quoting a player who had asked to remain anonymous, that Lasorda had lost control of his team. Whether that was accurate is beside the point. I was a rookie baseball writer and should not have relied on a single anonymous source on which to build a story.

It was a Sunday, the last game of a series with the Phillies in Philadelphia. Lasorda learned of my story when Yankees manager Billy Martin, with his team in Anaheim, California, for a series against the Angels, read it and phoned Lasorda to tell him about it. Lasorda angrily confronted me in the clubhouse after the Dodgers– Phillies game, wanting to know who my source was.

I couldn't betray a source, which further enraged him. Meanwhile, the team was headed home to Los Angeles for the All-Star break, while Lasorda, the National League manager, and a few of his players who were on the All-Star team, were headed to Seattle for the All-Star Game. We were flying commercial there, and Lasorda started up again with me at the airport, and again on the airplane once we were airborne. I finally told him that at that point he was invading my privacy, that if he wished to continue the one-sided conversation to do so the following day at the Kingdome in Seattle.

He was not happy. Our relationship was irrevocably strained from that point forward. When I introduced him to my future wife,

Marlene, a few years later, he said to her in all seriousness, "What are you doing with him? You can do better." I'll concede that point.

Yet for all his failings, while noting that we're all sinners in need of redemption, I prefer to believe that Lasorda is in heaven now. I sincerely hope so. He was raised in the Catholic church, attending Holy Savior in his hometown of Norristown, Pennsylvania, went to a Catholic elementary school, and regularly attended Mass throughout his life. He often told a story—perhaps apocryphal, given his inclination to not let facts get in the way of a good story—of attending Mass one Sunday morning in Cincinnati, when the Dodgers were in town to play the Reds, managed by John McNamara, another faithful Catholic who also was in attendance at that Mass. I should note that I was on the Angels beat when McNamara was their manager, and I thoroughly enjoyed working with him. We had a great relationship.

Lasorda's account is that when the Mass concluded, he saw McNamara stroll over to an altar where he lit a votive candle and kneeled in prayer. After McNamara left the church, Lasorda said he walked over and blew out the candle that McNamara had lit. Tom Hoffarth, an old newspaper friend of mine then writing for *Angelus News*, picks up the story, via an interview with Lasorda:

"And all during the game, I kept hollering at McNamara: 'It ain't gonna work, John, I blew out the candle.'"

That day, the Dodgers routed the Reds, 13-2. Lasorda admitted to McNamara what he had done.

That winter, Lasorda got a phone call from McNamara, who was on a trip to Rome.

"He told me, 'Try blowing this one out,'" Lasorda said.

Lasorda was a manager, yes, and a Hall of Fame one who took the job seriously, who hated losing even more than he disliked me, but he also was a showman, and even showmen can get to heaven. I am hopeful that that includes Lasorda.

The counter to Lasorda during my Dodgers tenure was a choirboy by comparison, the Dodgers' beloved broadcaster Vin Scully. I use *choirboy* affectionately, though having been privileged to know Vin he undoubtedly would wince at the description. But he too was a practicing Catholic, and seemingly existed on a higher plane than the rest of us, and I would be stunned if I were to learn that he ever uttered a single expletive, unless he did so when stepping barefoot on one of his grandkids' Legos. I'm guessing God readily would forgive that transgression.

The point is that Scully was one of the finest men any of us has ever met, myself included. I last saw him in April of 2015. By then, our daughter Hannah was of an age that she had begun to notice that some baseball players were "cute." I had not noticed that myself, so I'll take her word for it. She insisted I take her to a game. So my wife and I took her to a Rockies game at Dodger Stadium. About the third inning, I went to the press box, and between innings, I had a quick visit with Scully in his broadcast booth. All he wanted to talk about was Jordan Spieth's victory in the Masters the week before. In his storied career, Vin once was part of CBS Sports' Masters broadcast team.

This is not breaking news, by the way, but Vin Scully was a better man than he was a broadcaster, and as broadcasters go, he was unequivocally the best.

Yet more importantly, he was a man of strong faith. "I don't believe I ever saw him miss Mass on the road," his long-time Dodgers broadcast partner Ross Porter told me. "He somehow would always get to Mass on Sunday mornings before a game or go on Saturday night. Never missed. At home he never missed, either."

Porter gave his partner an accolade few of us—maybe none of us —could ever match. "I say this about Vin," he said. "I was with him for twenty-eight years. I was with him in so many tough situations when people were asking him for autographs or photographs, telling him stories, yet Vin always smiled. In twenty-eight years I never saw

Vin Scully be rude to one person. And I've said this: I think Vin Scully was most popular man in California."

Scully was even approached once about running for governor of California, Ross said. He noted that Los Angeles city councilwoman Rosalyn Wyman, who had had a role in bringing the Dodgers to Los Angeles from Brooklyn, was married to Eugene Wyman, the Democrat Party Chairman in California.

"Gene said to Vin, 'I'd like to take you to lunch,'" Porter said. "They go in and Gene Wyman said, 'Vin, I'm here on behalf of everyone in our party at the top and we're asking you to run for governor.' Vin told me, 'I knew about three seconds after he said that what the answer would be.' This was typical of Vin. He said, 'Gene, this is a great honor. Let me think about it and I'll call you in twenty-four hours.' He did and said, 'I just told him I was grateful I was made this offer, but I'm doing what I want to do, Gene, and I'd like to continue to do it. But thank you so much for the invitation.'

"Then he laughed and said to me, 'what Gene didn't know is that I am a Republican.'"

Scully, as Porter noted, was incapable of being rude to anyone, even political opponents.

Ross, in retirement, has done a series of interviews on YouTube, called *Ross Porter Sports Videos*. His best, he said, was his interview of Scully. His first question was about "your character, unblemished, undiminished. What is the source of your strength?"

"I guess in one word it would be faith," Scully replied. "I started out as a little boy groomed as a Roman Catholic. My mother was a very, very deeply religious person. Faith has helped me a great deal with my own personal tragedies."

Those tragedies include the 1994 death of his thirty-three-year-old son Michael, an engineering supervisor for Four Corners Pipe Line Inc., a subsidiary of Arco Oil Company, in a helicopter crash. Twenty-two years earlier, in 1972, his first wife Joan had died at thirty-five.

"I guess the two worst things that could happen to a human being, I believe, would be the loss of a wife and the loss of a child," he told Porter. "I experienced both of those pains. They never really go away. There's always a constant reminder of what was and what is no longer. Fortunately in the depths of despair God was kind enough to give me my [second] wife Sandy, our children, our sixteen grandchildren, plus the fact that he's allowed me to do what I love to do and has given me the health and longevity to do it all these years. Again, we get back to faith and the gifts I have been given to pull me out of what would have been a pretty despairing life.

"I know that everything I have is a gift, a gift from God. I firmly and truly believe that, and as long as you believe that I don't know how the ego can get involved. I spend every day sometime along the way saying, 'Dear God, thank you.' I don't know why I've been given these gifts. I didn't remember doing anything to deserve them, and yet I've been given them. So I certainly can't puff up about it. It's just been an unbelievable gift for which I'm eternally grateful."

Vin Scully's example on how to live a Christian life with humility and unambiguity as to where he stands with God is a lesson for all of us, with or without the audience he had.

I was an active baseball writer for twenty years, from 1978 through 1997, among other sports I covered, notably golf, and I was a full-time baseball writer for six of those twenty years, three with the Dodgers, three with the California Angels. Christianity often surfaced in varied ways, sometimes humorously so, for instance, a story of the Dodgers' third basemen at the time, Pedro Guerrero. Pedro was no facsimile of the great Baltimore Orioles' third baseman Brooks Robinson, who was known as the Human Vacuum Cleaner for his fielding prowess. One night in the ninth inning of a close game in which the Dodgers were leading, Guerrero was playing third with runners in scoring position, and Steve Sax, with his scattershot arm that at the time was a threat to fans sitting in the box seats directly behind first base, was playing second. After the game, Guerrero was asked what he was thinking.

"First, I pray to God that nobody hits the ball to me," he said. "Then I pray to God that nobody hits the ball to Steve Sax."

Then there was the legendary interchange between Baltimore

Orioles outfielder Pat Kelly and his Hall of Fame manager Earl Weaver. Kelly had decided to go into the ministry and thought that his manager should know. "Earl," he said, "I'm going to walk with the Lord."

Replied Weaver, "I'd rather you walk with the bases loaded."

Yes, baseball is a funny game, as the popular baseball man Joe Garagiola noted in the title of a book he authored.

But it also is a serious game, one that has been intertwined with Christianity probably since Abner Doubleday, as legend has it, introduced a rudimentary form of the game in Cooperstown, New York, in 1839. There was Billy Sunday, who played nine years in the National League, from 1882 to 1890, then became a renowned evangelist. "The devil says I'm out, but the Lord says I'm safe," he would say. Fire-and-brimstone was his specialty, and he routinely delivered it with a vigor that put fannies in the seats, as the old saying goes. One of his most memorable statements was that "going to church doesn't make you a Christian any more than going to a garage makes you an automobile."

Baseball has since been played throughout the years by a multitude of Christian men, many of whom might come as a surprise to some. I was fortunate to have known Reggie Jackson from my years on the Angels beat, fortunate because there was no player more entertaining and interesting day in and day out. He was great copy, as we said in the newspaper business. We never knew one day to the next which Reggie we might encounter. One day he was humble Reggie. The next day he was profane Reggie, or maybe arrogant Reggie. The day after he might be religious Reggie. But he was never uninteresting Reggie. I was blessed to know all the iterations of Reggie.

Five years after his retirement, he was working for the Yankees, who were in Anaheim to play the Angels. Long before the game, Jackson was talking to a few of us in the Yankees' dugout, and he was lamenting the fact that Joe DiMaggio no longer would don a uniform to participate in Old-Timers' Days. "He thinks he's the Pope," Jackson said, though there might have been a distasteful adjective that began with the letter *f* preceding Pope. I later wrote in jest (at least I was hoping he would recognize that it was in jest) that that bothered Reggie, because he thought *he* was the Pope.

At that point, though, I was certain we had a good enough relationship that he'd take it for which it was intended—a joke. When I began covering golf, I did not see him much. I ran into him at Pebble Beach Golf Links one year when he was playing in the AT&T Pebble Beach Pro-Am. Then, at least twenty years after he had retired, I ran into him at the Butch Harmon School of Golf in Las Vegas. I was there to see Butch, who was introducing a line of golf shafts. Jackson, residing in Las Vegas at the time, was there for a lesson from Harmon, who generally is recognized as the best golf instructor in the world. Reggie looked as fit as ever, so I asked him what compelled him to keep working out so hard.

"Vanity," he replied.

So it went with Reggie.

All those years with access to one of the most interesting and intelligent athletes in history, it never occurred to me to discuss Christianity with him. Then one night, television journalist Charlie Rose, on his eponymous PBS show, *Charlie Rose,* had Jackson as a guest. He asked Reggie what his life was like.

"It's wonderful," Jackson replied.

Why?

"Mostly because, I think, I'm grateful and thankful. I thank God every day, as often as I can during the day. If you thank God for all the things that you are thankful for—your eyesight, your nice home, the sandwich you had, the nice car you drive, your friends, your family—you'd run out of daylight before you would get to the end. And if you do start thanking him, you'll be happier, if you give thanks."

I believe that he was sincere, knowing him as I do. He always seemed to provide honest answers, whatever the questions and potential backlash. He was exceedingly intelligent and open to revelatory introspection, depending on his mood. In 2012, Phil Taylor wrote a great story on Jackson for *Sports Illustrated*, one that delved into his faith.

"Jackson knows what makes for a sexy story and what makes reporters turn their tape recorders off, and so he gives a warning," Taylor wrote. "'This is going to make people roll their eyes,' he says, 'but I'm going to talk about God.'"

He opened up about his faith journey, which began as often is the case with the revelation that there must be more to this life. It began seven years earlier, according to Taylor's story, when he was in an automobile accident in Tampa, Florida, his car rear-ended, causing it to roll over several times. "He walked away with only minor injuries," Taylor wrote, "'but it was God tapping me on the shoulder,' he says. 'It makes you think about your purpose, about His plan for you.'"

Jackson sought counsel from other Christians, notably Mike Singletary, then the San Francisco 49ers head coach. He began reading his Bible with greater frequency. Taylor concluded the part of his story dealing with Jackson's faith with this: "Most of Jackson's mornings now begin with five-mile walks on the beach, good for both his body and soul. He has an iPhone alarm set to ring every day at 6:30 a.m., reminding him to read the daily entry on the [Android] app *Jesus Said*."

A year later, in 2013, Jim Mandelaro of the Rochester, New York, newspaper the *Democrat & Chronicle,* asked Jackson in an interview whether he was glad he had played for Billy Martin, when the latter managed the Yankees. The two had had a famously contentious relationship. "I would say no," Jackson replied. "I wouldn't say I enjoyed that, or I'm glad I did it. As a Christian, God is always working with you and putting you in situations to improve and shape you to be the person he wants you to be. Would I volunteer for it? No. Am I glad it happened? Probably. But I would not want to do it again."

I was fortunate to have had a great relationship with him. I will even forgive him for sticking me with the cab fare when he encountered me hailing a taxi outside the Hyatt Regency in Milwaukee prior to game three of the American League Championship Series in 1982. We rode out to County Stadium together, and when we arrived, he said, "I'm running late. Can you pick this up?"

For baseball writers, he was the most interesting player of that era to cover, by a wide margin, too, and it thrills me that he has allowed God to enter his life in a meaningful way, and is now open to speaking about it.

Given my own quiet faith journey, I'm in no position to fault him for not being more open about his Christian walk, assuming he had one, earlier in his life. Of course, there often was an inherent bias against Christianity infiltrating baseball clubhouses. Christianity over the years had proven to be a dubious asset from managers' perspective, whatever the level of baseball. Case in point was Rick Duncan, a former Vanderbilt University star, minor league player, and Christian, who in an unbylined story on Vanderbilt's website, recalled a coach who said, "I'll tell you what we don't need on this team. We don't need milkshake drinkers. We need beer drinkers on this team. If you want to win, we need beer drinkers."

"I thought 'okay, I know who you are talking to,'" Duncan said.

Another coach once said to him, "The problem with this team is it's a Sunday school class." Duncan later said, "I was thinking to myself that the problem with this team is we don't have a shortstop."

Baseball history is rife with managers who preferred players whose post-game refreshments were eighty-proof or higher over those headed to the malt shop and to church on Sundays. The Hall of Fame manager Casey Stengel was among them. "They say some of my stars drink whiskey, but I have found that ones who drink milkshakes don't win many ball games," he famously said. Stengel's successor as the Yankees' manager, Ralph Houk, concurred. "I'll take nine whiskey drinkers over nine milkshake drinkers any day," Houk said in 1960.

The irony is that the Yankees' stellar double-play duo in those days featured shortstop Tony Kubek and second baseman Bobby Richardson, teetotalers and Christians known as the Milkshake Twins. Early in Richardson's career, Stengel said, "Look at him. He doesn't drink, he doesn't smoke, he doesn't chew, he doesn't stay out late, and he still can't hit .250." Yet both Richardson and Kubek eventually became all-stars. The Yankees, meanwhile, won the American League pennant in seven of Kubek's nine years and seven of Richardson's ten years with the team, suggesting that Stengel, Houk, and others, on this front, at least, had no idea what they were talking about.

Another of Stengel's players, the tempestuous and aforementioned Billy Martin, was interviewed by the legendary *Sports Illustrated* writer Frank Deford and told him this story:

> "Yeah, there was this time he called a team meeting. 'Now, first, you lovers,' [Stengel] began. 'You single guys who are out chasing something all night and you married guys who are telling the girls you're single.' We thought he was gonna stop there. But he went on. 'And you drinkers'—Case was getting some guys more than once—'I'm the only one who is gonna stay up all night drinking.' Everybody was sure he was through then, but he went on. 'And you churchgoers and milkshake drinkers. Now, it's fine to have some of you guys on a team, but if you don't start showing me some guts out there, if you don't play hard enough for me, I'm going to make every one of you go out and get a double Scotch and a woman.' Oh, he got everybody that time, Casey did. He didn't mention a name, and he got the whole team.'"

The straight and narrow, occupied largely by Christians, often has been the road less traveled in baseball, and on those occasions when it was traveled the ride was often bumpy, as the Texas Rangers learned in the late nineties. That team, then only recently having been owned by a future president of the United States, George W. Bush, was constructed with a careful eye on players' character, which often included their Christian faith. Bush openly defended this approach, no doubt contributing to the backlash. A decade or so later, the Colorado Rockies similarly built a team with more character than characters, and even played well enough to advance to their first World Series. Yet there were those who considered too much Christianity in a clubhouse a potential liability.

In July of 1997, Chris Smith authored a three-thousand-word story in the *New York Times Magazine* titled, "God is an .800 Hitter." It was a reasonably balanced account of the Texas Rangers, notwithstanding a headline that made no sense whatsoever. Wouldn't God be a 1.000 hitter? Nothing in the story ties it to the headline other than a mention of God, suggesting to me that the *New York Times Magazine* editor or headline writer did not understand Christianity.

The story generally was about Christianity in the clubhouse, specifically in the Rangers' clubhouse. Then Texas Governor Bush, at that point no longer the owner, was explaining to Smith that the Rangers "won a lot of games over the years, but we'd never made the playoffs. . . Maybe we're missing something.

"We were focused on talent alone, but you build a team around common values and teamwork. The question we asked was, 'Does character matter?' We said it does. Then we made decisions based on that."

Among the decisions was to hire a born-again Christian Johnny Oates to manage the Rangers. "Texans love values—they're down to earth, they care about honoring their neighbor, respecting others, loyalty to a wife—and Johnny Oates personifies that," Bush said. "Texans are proud to support a decent, down-to-earth guy."

Smith then wrote:

But can't we let baseball be baseball? "I don't know about other cities," Bush says acidly, "but values still matter in Texas.". . .

"Can a ball club be a force for morals and values?" asks Bush, who helped launch the Rangers' conversion and still sounds very much like an owner. "Yes it can—and here's why it can. People pay attention to stars—what happens on the

field, and in this day and age, particularly what happens off
the field. And a team can emphasize values, like you're
seeing here today. We know no one's perfect. But we demand
decent standards of behavior from our players on the
Rangers."

One might assume that whatever the profession, other maybe
than the proverbially oldest profession, employees with strong
morals and values would be preferred over scoundrels. One would
not be wrong to assume that, but when those players who espouse
these morals and values and do so from a faith-based position, well,
the old argument about managers preferring whiskey drinkers to
milkshake drinkers resurfaces, albeit with a different spin.

The Colorado Rockies, an expansion team that debuted in 1993,
created controversies and headlines in 2006 for their efforts to intro-
duce morals and values into their clubhouse. Dave Zirin, writing in
the far-left publication *The Nation*, took on the issue with a story
headlined, "The Rockies Pitch Religion." The headline itself was
innocuous, but the first paragraph dispelled any notion that the story
was going to be fair and balanced, to borrow from one cable news
network's slogan:

> In Colorado, there stands a holy shrine called Coors Field. On
> this site, named for the holiest of beers, a team plays that has
> been chosen by Jesus Christ himself to play .500 baseball in
> the National League West. And if you don't believe me, just
> ask the manager, the general manager and the team's owner.

Zirin was writing in response to a *USA TODAY* story, written by
an old friend from my newspaper days, Bob Nightengale, and headlined, "Baseball's Rockies seek revival on two levels." Zirin began
his story with a full tank of snark that was empty by the end of it. For
instance, character, "according to the Tribe of Coors," Zirin wrote,
"means accepting Jesus Christ as your personal lord and savior. . .
"The Rockies right now," he wrote, "are a noxious reflection of a

time in US history when generals speak of crusades and the President recounts his personal conversations with Yahweh. ('You're doing a heckuva job, Goddy!)." That was a rather juvenile reference, falling far short of the "witty" denunciation of Bush that Zirin presumably intended, based on the former president's praise of FEMA chairman Michael Brown for his leadership in the wake of Hurricane Katrina when he said, "Brownie, you're doing a heck of a job."

In the vernacular of baseball, that was a swing and a miss.

Zirin also mentioned how other teams were embracing Christianity, including the Atlanta Braves, who held Faith Days. Of course, Faith Days have been a promotion for years, same as Bat Day or Cap Day, designed to attract spectators. Many minor and major league teams hold Faith Days to bolster attendance. After one of Atlanta's Faith Days games, Braves pitcher John Smoltz, now in the National Baseball Hall of Fame, gave a testimonial about his Christian faith.

Smoltz ran afoul of Zirin, joining good company in the process: Charlie Monfort, the Chairman and CEO of the Rockies; Dan O'Dowd, the club's general manager; and Clint Hurdle, the Rockies' manager. "If Monfort, O'Dowd and Hurdle want to pray on their own time, more power to them," Zirin wrote. "But the ballpark isn't a church. Smoltz isn't a preacher. And fans aren't a flock. Instead of using their position of commercial power to field a God Squad, the Rockies might want to think about getting some decent players. There was once this guy named Babe Ruth. Not too much for the religion, and his character was less than sterling. But I hear he could play some decent ball."

The first paragraph of the *USA TODAY* story to which Zirin was responding was this: "No copies of *Playboy* or *Penthouse* are in the clubhouse of baseball's Colorado Rockies. There's not even a *Maxim*. The only reading materials are daily newspapers, sports and car magazines and the Bible."

One could reasonably argue that neither *Playboy* nor *Penthouse* ever warranted being called "reading material," but so be it. The fact is that every baseball clubhouse had those kinds of magazines scattered about at one time, and this even after female sportswriters first gained entry into clubhouses. Presumably, ridding those kinds of publications from clubhouses was long overdue.

The story continued: "Music filled with obscenities, wildly popular with youth today and in many other clubhouses, is not played. A player will curse occasionally but usually in hushed tones. Quotes from Scripture are posted in the weight room. Chapel service is packed on Sundays. Prayer and fellowship groups each Tuesday are well-attended. It's not unusual for the front office executives to pray together.

"On the field, the Rockies are trying to make the playoffs for the first time in 11 seasons and only the second time in their 14-year history. Behind the scenes, they quietly have become an organization guided by Christianity—open to other religious beliefs but embracing a Christian-based code of conduct they believe will bring them focus and success."

It did indeed bring them success. A year later, the Rockies reached the World Series for the first time in franchise history, and the controversy regained momentum.

Mollie Hemingway is a bestselling author, editor in chief of the *Federalist*, a Fox News contributor, a Christian, the daughter of a Lutheran pastor, and a woman I admire. She is a St. Louis Cardinals fan who grew up in Colorado and was still there when Denver was awarded an expansion team, the Colorado Rockies.

Hemingway, writing for *Get Religion* at the time, took on the critics, including Vince Bzdek of the *Washington Post*, who had written a story headlined, "You've Gotta Have Faith? Colorado Rockies at Play in the Fields of the Lord." Hemingway called the story "craptacular." She noted that Bzdek wrote that "several players have crosses dangling from their necks," that "Ramon Ortiz. . . makes the sign of the cross on his way to the mound."

"You know why the newspaper biz is doing so poorly?" Hemingway wrote. "Not enough snark against religious people. I'm glad Bzdek is here to rescue the fishwrappers from obscurity. I mean, maybe not in the *Washington Post* newsroom, but making the sign of the cross and cross pendants aren't exactly unheard of in America."

Hemingway concluded her story with this: "Newsrooms don't need to put the worst possible construction on a team just because some of them are Christian and actually care about doing their jobs as Christians. Perhaps the *Washington Post* even has a few Christians in its newsrooms who care about character and teamwork. It could happen."

A standing ovation is warranted for that conclusion from Hemingway.

An argument could be made that baseball might have benefitted from more Christianity in the clubhouse, not less. In 1970, journeyman pitcher Jim Bouton's landmark book, *Ball Four*, opened the clubhouse doors and provided baseball fans a behind-the-scenes look at life in the big leagues, warts and all, the warts helping make it a monumental bestseller. It exposed the dark side of the game—the widespread wantonness, drunkenness, and amphetamine use, greenies, as they were called. The promiscuity involved what were called "baseball Annies" (hence Kevin Costner's love interest in the baseball film *Bull Durham* was named Annie). The rampant debauchery apparently helped break up the grind of a 162-game season.

The book received remarkably good reviews, its outliers few. Among the latter was the review by renowned New York baseball columnist Dick Young, who called Bouton "a social leper." *New York Times* writer Robert Lipsyte's review, meanwhile, included this: "Bouton's anecdotes and insights are enlightening, hilarious and, most important, unavailable elsewhere. They breathe a new life into a game choked by pontificating statisticians, image-conscious officials and scared ballplayers."

I confess, again, that I am a sinner in need of salvation, but I gleefully read the book at the time and discussed it at length, probing for confirmation of its authenticity, with a minor league player who in his off season worked for my father in the sporting goods business.

But back to Lipsyte's review. "Image-conscious," I submit, ought to be viewed as a positive rather than a pejorative.

Mark McLemore, a second baseman and a Christian on that

Texas Rangers' team to which George W. Bush alluded, adamantly insisted that living their values should not have been viewed as pros- elytizing. "Parents are looking at us—professional athletes—to solve their problems with their kids," he told the *New York Times* reporter. "And we can't do that. Athletes have realized that, hey, here's another avenue to get to kids, to get to people, to get to the public, and let them know that we're real, vulnerable people."

In the face of anti-Christianity vitriol, the Bible, not surprisingly, informs on how to respond. Paul wrote, "What then shall we say to these things? If God is for us, who can be against us?" (Romans 8:31 ESV). And we're instructed to defend our faith: "But in your hearts honor Christ the Lord as holy, always being prepared to make a defense to anyone who asks you for a reason for the hope that is in you; yet do it with gentleness and respect" (1 Peter 3:15 ESV).

Zirin, incidentally, used Babe Ruth to make a point that talent was more important than character, that though Ruth was something of a scoundrel not much interested in religion, he was a standout player, one of the best of all time. Accordingly, Ruth was one of the five players in the inaugural class inducted into the National Baseball Hall of Fame in 1936.

But so was pitcher Christy Mathewson, who won 373 games in his career, third on the all-time list, and had a career earned run average of 2.13, ninth best in history. Mathewson was a devout Christian.

"He set a high moral code," Philadelphia A's manager Connie Mack told the *Daily Boston Globe*. "He was lauded by the churches, ministers used his career as sermon topics, he gave dignity and char- acter to baseball. . . he was the greatest pitcher who ever lived."

Acknowledging that a flamboyant rogue, Babe Ruth, makes for better newspaper copy, I would also submit that Mathewson was a better role model, who more than a century ago set a standard that Christian athletes today would do well to emulate. He carried a Bible with him on road trips and honored a vow he made to his mother, to never pitch on Sundays, the latter realistically not a viable option these days, of course.

Consider this, too, that not only is Mathewson enshrined in the National Baseball Hall of Fame in Cooperstown, New York, along with the usual accoutrements from his career, including gloves and balls, but it also has his Bible, "a tattered, leather-bound 'Sunday School Teacher's Edition Bible,'" according to the Hall of Fame.

In the book, *Christy Mathewson, the Christian Gentleman: How One Man's Faith and Fastball Forever Changed Baseball*, author Bob Gaines wrote of Mathewson's boyhood pastor, John Howard Harris: "Harris was energetic, physically fit, a dynamic orator who mixed powerful intellect with a resounding faith. As a child, Christy always sat in the front row, eagerly listening to every word from the pulpit."

Mathewson was an early example of an athlete living out his Christian faith in public life, without compromise, and witnessing by setting a standard that did not go unnoticed at the time even without the benefit of television or the internet. He showed that it is possible to be great, an immortal even, without hewing to others' lower standards that might include a measure of depravity that garners them greater attention.

Better to follow Christy's example than Babe's and to remember that a baseball field, in reality or in film, as great as the game is, is not the promised land, as this exchange in *Field of Dreams* reminded us.

"Is this heaven?" Shoeless Joe asked Ray.

"No," Ray replied. "It's Iowa."

SIX

The Sound-Bite Witness

I GREW up in an age when newspapers were ubiquitous, many major cities even having more than one. When I was on the Dodgers beat, I believe there were at least seven newspapers traveling with the team. Local television stations featured ten-minute sports reports on the evening news. Yet the sum of these entities still did not allow any real opportunities for Christian athletes to profess their faith, even if they were inclined to do so. An old friend from a competing newspaper often said only partly in jest that we were just filling up the space between the ads. The truth in his quip was that newspaper stories are confined to limited space and subject to editing by editors more likely predisposed to avoiding Christian references. And sports segments on the evening news provided mostly scores and highlights and short interviews.

There was no cable television in those days, hence no cable stations airing games. There was no internet, either, hence no social media. Occasionally, we'd learn of an athlete's faith, though it was rare. When our family moved to Southern California and I briefly became an Angels fan, I remember hearing that center fielder Albie Pearson was a devout Christian, one who eventually became a pastor and started a ministry in the Coachella Valley in Southern California. There, too, was Dodgers pitcher Sandy Koufax, a practicing Jew, who opted out of pitching the first game of the World Series in 1965 because it fell on Yom Kippur. But otherwise, an athlete's faith largely went unnoticed or at least unmentioned.

That was then. This is now.

The information superhighway, also known as the World Wide Web, came along, as did cable television, social media, and now live-streaming. The number of cable television networks exploded, reminding me, as one who is not a television junkie (aside from sports and news), of the Bruce Springsteen song, "57 Channels (and Nothing On)." In time, every major college football and basketball game, every NFL, NBA, and Major League Baseball game, and every PGA Tour and LPGA Tour event were televised somewhere, and all included live post-game interviews that cannot be edited. The internet, as it evolved, played a huge role, too, with the expanding number of social media platforms, notably Twitter, Facebook, and Instagram. The opportunities for athletes to represent themselves as Christians, to witness in accordance with the Biblical command to do so, exploded.

Obviously, a post-game sermon delivered by an athlete who was instrumental to a team's victory, however eloquently delivered, will not play well with audiences. It is said that brevity is the soul of wit. And of a Christian witness, we might add. Attention spans are short these days, but fortunately so are sound bites.

It brings to mind the simple children's song written long before Twitter and Facebook, before cable television or the internet, that is applicable in the age we live in, a lesson in how Christians can witness without a great deal of effort or time, while allowing the Holy Spirit to come off the bench and do his work. Here are the lyrics:

> This little light of mine,
> I'm gonna let it shine.

> This little light of mine,
> I'm gonna let it shine.
> This little light of mine,
> I'm gonna let it shine,
> Let it shine, let it shine, oh let it shine

This ditty describes a child-like faith. As Paul wrote, "For at one time you were darkness, but now you are light in the Lord. Walk as children of light" (Ephesians 5:8 ESV). Christians are biblically implored not to keep their faith to themselves. It is God's will that we shine a light on it. And with television cameras rolling, with recorders recording, it can be done so easily, so effortlessly, (yet still not always so appreciatively), and one needn't be an evangelist or a Biblical scholar to do so. The only requirement is to be a child of God. As Jesus explained to his disciples:

> At that time the disciples came to Jesus, saying, "Who is the greatest in the kingdom of heaven?" And calling to him a child, he put him in the midst of them and said, "Truly, I say to you, unless you turn and become like children, you will never enter the kingdom of heaven. Whoever humbles himself like this child is the greatest in the kingdom of heaven." (Matthew 18:1–4 ESV)

When opportunities present themselves in public settings, which I define as interviews, pre- or post-game, do what Joe Mazzulla, the head coach of the Boston Celtics, did while still the interim head coach. Mazzulla is a Christian who is demonstrably unafraid of letting his light shine. When the United Kingdom's Prince and Princess of Wales were in Boston in the fall of 2022 and attended a Celtics game at the TD Garden, a reporter asked Mazzulla about them. "Did you get a chance to meet with the royal family, and if not, what was it like having them there in the building?"

"Jesus, Mary, and Joseph?" Mazzulla asked.

"The Prince and Princess of Wales," the reporter replied, chuckling.

"Oh, no, I did not," Mazzulla said. "I'm only familiar with one royal family. I don't know too much about that one. But I hope they're Celtics fans."

Mazzulla had delivered a master class in soundbite witnessing, using the platform available to him at that moment in time to do what the song says, and what Jesus himself said: "Let your light shine before others, that they may see your good deeds and glorify your Father in heaven" (Matthew 5:16 NIV). It was unplanned, certainly unscripted, but not unnoticed. I Googled "Mazzulla" and "Wales" at the time and it showed 337,000 results.

Soundbite witnessing is a variation of what is known as the elevator pitch—when you're in an elevator and have, say, thirty seconds to explain something to someone before the elevator stops and they disembark. Here is how Praise & Proclaim Ministries describes the elevator pitch, as it applies to Christian testimony:

> Alone in an elevator, another person steps in and presses a button for the 12th floor. An angel of the Lord taps you on the shoulder and whispers that you have thirty seconds to proclaim the gospel before they step out.
>
> What would you say? . . .
>
> We live in a time where technology dominates our culture and convenience permeates our decision-making. Christians with a desire to proclaim the gospel may only be provided with a small window of opportunity.
>
> Perhaps Christians ought to consider preparing themselves with an elevator witness to tell others what Christ has already done for us.[1]

Having an audience, of course, is essential, and Christian

athletes, the stars, at least, have large audiences built into their everyday lives. Every game always includes a post-game interview, as well as an opportunity for the Christian athlete to express his or her faith via social media. C. J. Stroud, Ohio State University's star quarterback, a Heisman Trophy finalist in 2022, had more than 19,000 followers on his Facebook fan page. Ohio State, undefeated and ranked number one in the country entering its game with arch-rival Michigan in November of 2022, lost to the Wolverines, 45-23. It was an extraordinarily difficult loss given the Buckeyes' exceedingly high expectations that included their winning the national championship. Stroud took the loss hard, as one might expect, but he also provided a remarkable degree of maturity and Christian perspective on his Facebook fan page.

> "If you want excuses," he wrote, "we don't have those. If you want tears—keep looking. Priceless are the moments where you are given the opportunity to learn from your defeats. But those are the moments where one can grow the most.

> "Romans 5:3–5 says 'More than that, we rejoice in our sufferings, knowing that suffering produces endurance, and endurance produces character, and character produces hope, and hope does not put us to shame, because God's love has been poured into our hearts through the Holy Spirit who has been given to us.'"

Simple, emotional, from the heart, and from the Bible, Stroud, with his enormous stature in his sport, briefly and eloquently used that platform to keep Christ front and center, with the ability to influence and embolden others to step out in faith.

On the downside. . . yes, there often is a downside. None of us is perfect, so those who do step out in faith open themselves to accusations of hypocrisy should they step out of line. I offer two legendary Christians addressing that dilemma.

Billy Sunday, the former nineteenth century baseball player

turned evangelist, said, "Hypocrites in the Church? Yes, and in the lodge and at the home. Don't hunt through the Church for a hypocrite. Go home and look in the mirror. Hypocrites? Yes. See that you make the number one less."

Charles Spurgeon, the renowned nineteenth-century preacher, said: "I heard one man say that he did not believe there was a true Christian living, because he had found so many hypocrites. I reminded him that there could be no hypocrites if there were no genuine Christians. No one would try to forge bank notes if there were no genuine ones."

Claims of hypocrisy are the lament of Christians everywhere because we are all sinners. Golden State Warriors star Steph Curry experienced this first hand in a 2017 game when he thought he was fouled and in anger threw his mouthpiece at, or at least in the general direction of, a referee. He was ejected from the game, inviting a Twitter faction to point out his hypocrisy. To his credit, Curry tweeted this: "No excuse for that! Gotta remember who I am playing for. . ."

Brian Smith, writing for *Athletes In Action*'s website, expertly came to the defense of Curry.

> "Unfortunately, this stand-off represents a similar script for any Christian athlete who stumbles—let alone one with such an enormous platform," Smith wrote. "Given the frequency of this occurrence, we desperately need some perspective. Without it, we will continue spinning together in the same hamster wheel of craziness.

> "Taking the posture of 'a real Christian would not/should not do that or he is such a hypocrite' becomes a dangerous position to hold, evidencing a failure of perspective on multiple levels.

> "Romans 3:23 is pretty clear when it says 'For all have sinned and fall short of the glory of God.' Athletes fall under

the category of 'all' too. We can be hopeful that the Christian athletes we cheer for will refrain from sin and strive towards obedience. We can even be disappointed when they fall short. But to have a heart of anger that self-righteously screams (or even whispers) 'Some Christian he is' shows a misunder-standing of our human nature."[2]

That Christians are sinners, too, is not a revelation, though there are those who are all too willing to pretend it is while using it as a cudgel in an attempt to silence them.

Sarah Stonestreet of the Colson Center, in a video episode of *What Would You Say*, addressed the suggestion that hypocrisy should disqualify Christians from professing the word of God. The truncated version of her video is this: "The next time someone says, 'I don't go to church because the church is full of hypocrites,' remember these three things. Number one: hypocrisy requires a moral standard. Number two: Jesus condemned religious hypocrisy. Number three: the behaviors of the believers are not the litmus test for Christianity."

We're sinners and God forgives those who ask for forgiveness. End of story.

My sports fandom for teams largely has been weaned out of me over the years by the sportswriters' unwritten creed—no cheering in the press box. We rooted mostly for great story lines. The better the story line, the easier it was to write the story and the more readers it likely would attract. We also rooted, with deadlines looming, for short games and no extra innings or overtime.

So I've become more of a situational fan of teams and athletes. Among those teams and athletes were the Seattle Seahawks and their former quarterback Russell Wilson. Part of it is my northwest roots, though ordinarily I was indifferent to how the team played. Then they hired Pete Carroll to coach (I loved what he had done at the University of Southern California, my wife's alma mater) and in 2012 drafted this undersized quarterback out of Wisconsin in the third round to whom Carroll gave the starting job from day one of his rookie season.

Wilson took the Seahawks to two Super Bowls, winning one of them, and was as much fun to watch as any player in the National Football League. Far more importantly, however, was that Wilson, nine times a Pro Bowl quarterback, a superstar however one defines it, put his Christian faith first and did so going back to his college days. And he did not need a pulpit, either.

Among his favorite Bible verses is Matthew 6:33, in which Jesus succinctly provides a blueprint on how one should live his life by putting Christ first: When Wilson signed autographs in college, he always added "Matthew 6:33."

"Whenever I do an autograph," he said during a Rose Bowl news conference in December 2011, "I write that scripture, Matthew 6:33: 'But seek first the kingdom of God and his righteousness all these things will be added unto you.' It's something that's helped me out throughout my life and my experiences."

He also has signed using John 3:30, John the Baptist speaking on putting Christ ahead of himself more often: "He must increase, but I must decrease."

Bearing witness cannot get simpler than a man signing his name and adding a Bible verse that likely will lead to the recipient of the autograph to consult a Bible to see what it says.

Teague McKamey, a Christian writer with a blog, *The Voice of One,* is a Seattle Seahawks fan who was about eleven years old when he stood in line for hours to get Seattle quarterback Jim Zorn's autograph. Zorn had a stack of photos of himself ready, grabbed one, signed his name, and added "John 3:16."

"My heart skipped a beat," McKamey wrote. "What did this verse say? Had Zorn picked it just for me? Could it be a key to understanding myself and my life? Once home, I scrambled to find my *Good News Bible*. Somehow, I managed to locate John 3:16."

"For God so loved the world. . . "

McKamey initially had "hoped to find some secret key that would unlock the mystery that was my self. But this verse wasn't about me at all. It just talked about Jesus." He was disappointed until he eventually realized that knowing Jesus was the whole point.

"I thought Zorn fumbled by writing John 3:16 under his autograph," McKamey wrote. "Now I know what a touchdown that was. He shared Jesus, who is God's will for my life, who is my high calling, who is my new life (Philippians. 3:14, Colossians. 3:4)."

Wilson was never timid about sharing his faith in interviews, perhaps most memorably having done so on media day prior to Super Bowl XLIX in the Phoenix area. "In terms of my legacy off the field," he said, "I want to be a Christian man that helps lead and helps change lives and helps serve other people. It's not about me, you know. It's not about me and it's about just helping other people. So that's kind of where I keep my focus.

"In terms of my faith, my faith is everything. God comes first, family and friends come second, and football comes third. I think when you keep it in that order, great things happen to you. You don't stress out about much."

And, finally, and not as an afterthought, he said, "I'm able to use my gift to glorify God. That's what it's all about for me."

These weren't soundbites, but close enough, and he had used the Super Bowl platform, the most important stage in American sports, to declare his faith to an audience of reporters, some of whom actually might have kept from rolling their eyes and then recounting Wilson's statements of faith to their audiences back home. One can hope.

Philadelphia Eagles quarterback Nick Foles, meanwhile, gave a brilliant soundbite testimony to the largest audience in American sports, moments after leading the Eagles to a 41-33 victory over the New England Patriots in Super Bowl LII. Five seconds into his postgame interview broadcast around the world, Foles, the game's most valuable player, gave a textbook example of what we as Christians are called to do.

"Unbelievable," he said. "All glory to God. I wouldn't be out here without God, without Jesus in my life."

Later in the game's aftermath, in his news conference, he expounded on his faith. "I can tell you that first and foremost, I don't have the strength to come out here and play this game like that. And that's an everyday walk. We have struggles as people, and that's just been my rock. And my family."

His coach Doug Pederson similarly deflected the focus from himself to God. "I can only give the praise to my Lord and Savior Jesus Christ for giving me this opportunity."

Obviously there is no way to measure the impact, other than to note that the larger the audience the more likely it is to land on a great number of people, to touch their hearts as they wrestle with or ponder their own faith walk, to let the Holy Spirit work.

Social media, for all its flaws—unapologetically, I have referred to Twitter as a sewer on several occasions over the years and my opinion has not changed—has exponentially expanded opportunities to express one's faith, a perfect venue for the soundbite witness, 140 characters or fewer on Twitter initially. So has the expansion of televised sports that always include post-game interviews.

Among the best use of the post-game interview to bear witness to one's faith that I can recall came in the 2021 college football season in the wake of Texas A&M's remarkable upset victory over Alabama, the number-one ranked team in the country.

Seth Small, a kicker for Texas A&M's football team, kicked a twenty-eight-yard field goal as time expired to give the Aggies a wholly unexpected 41–38 victory before a crowd of more than 100,000 on hand at Kyle Field in College Station, Texas, and millions more watching on national television.

In a post-game interview, Small obviously was asked his reaction. Not so obvious was his response.

"It was probably the third best moment of my life," he said. "Right after I accepted Jesus into my heart as my true Lord and Savior, and then after getting married to my wife this summer, I'd rank this three."

It was a beautiful testimony, in two sentences.

Another phenomenal example of soundbite witnessing for Christ involves a man who by circumstance has been forced to emphasize sound in his life. His name is Jake Olson and he is blind.

The story of Jake Olson has been widely reported. At ten months, he had one eye removed because of cancer. He was twelve when the cancer infected his other eye, which then was removed, leaving him blind.

In April of 2015, I spoke to him for a story I did for GolfDigest.com, after learning that he played golf. He had been a recreational golfer, enjoying it, but not seriously committed to it, until Tiger Woods, as he did to so many others, mesmerized him with his victory in the U.S. Open in 2008 at Torrey Pines. As I wrote, the hook was set. Six months later, Olson had an opportunity to play Torrey Pines. "I fell in love with the game then and there," he told me. "It was really cool to play a course the caliber of Torrey Pines where Tiger had won. So I really wanted to start practicing hard and maybe make a professional career out of it one day."

He also told me that he had been playing decently, "for a twelve-year-old. Then I learned I would have to go blind."

Then I learned I would have to go blind.

Who among us can even comprehend that sentence and what it would mean? Who among us would not have been angry at God at that point?

Jake learned on October 1, 2009, that he would lose his second eye, that surgery was scheduled for November 12. He admitted that the thought tormented him, he told CNN, though he reconciled himself to a future without sight with a maturity well beyond his years.

Olson, meanwhile, had been a long-time fan of the University of Southern California football team, and when its coach at the time, Pete Carroll, heard of his plight, he befriended Jake and hosted him at Trojan practices. Jake went on to play football at Orange Lutheran High School, as its long-snapper on extra points and field-goal attempts. His desire was to attend USC and to do the same for the Trojans. He enrolled there as a business major and soon got the call, that he would be part of the team.

Coach Carroll ended up leaving to become the head coach of the Seattle Seahawks, but his successor at USC, Clay Helton, took up Jake's cause. The Trojans, ranked fourth in the country in 2017, opened against Western Michigan at the Los Angeles Memorial Coliseum. In advance of the game, Helton consulted with Western Michigan's head coach Tim Lester and proposed that when Western Michigan scored a touchdown that on the extra point the Trojans would not attempt to rush the kicker, and that when USC scored a touchdown that Western Michigan would reciprocate. Lester immediately agreed.

"I told them [his players] the entire situation," Lester said, "and said, 'you can't touch him, you can't yell at him, everyone get down so it looks like a football play, but nobody move. What we are about to do is bigger than the game. This is about what kind of people we want to be, what we represent. This is bigger than us.'"

Indeed. When the time came, Olson's snap was perfect and the kick was good.

"There was a beauty in it," Olson said afterwards. "If you can't see how God works things out, I think you're the blind one."

Jake Olson never lost his faith in the Lord and has gone on to become a motivational speaker, who uses the platforms available to him to share his faith, the best and most inspiring example of the soundbite witness. On March 21, 2023, Olson Tweeted this: "Lord fix my eyes on the things I can't see now. I live my life by faith, not by sight. For I humbly acknowledge the only certainty I have in this life is that you are God over all, and you have already given me all I could ever need in an eternity with you."

I have relied on words for my living, but only one came to me when I read this: Wow. He was quoting 2 Corinthians 5:7, "for we walk by faith, not by sight," a great Bible verse that was exponentially more impactful coming from a young man who is blind.

In a video online, Jake sums up succinctly and importantly what it means to be a Christian, whatever the hardships we might encounter. "At a young age," he said, "I learned that life will bring adversity and challenges. The biggest reason I have been able to overcome adversity and develop a positive attitude is because I have a strong faith in the Lord Jesus Christ. . . Even though the cancer took my eyes, it didn't take my will to go on and become the best I can be."

Even through his darkness, he can *see* what is most important in this life, and accordingly has become a beacon of faith, shining a light on it, doing so effectively in his motivational speeches and tweets, so that others might *see* it, too.

SEVEN

Does God Pick Winners?

WHEN I PLAYED BASEBALL, ambitiously yet without a commensurate degree of ability, I prayed before every game, even before every at bat, and I did so from Little League through to my senior year of varsity baseball in high school. But I never prayed for victory, only for God to protect me from injury and to allow me to play to the best of my ability. I occasionally suffered an injury, all of them minor, but on the latter request, to play to the best of my ability, he complied. My senior season of high school I hit .250, and needed a single in my last at bat to reach that baseball benchmark of mediocrity, the best of my ability.

But I've wondered, as many Christians no doubt have, whether God cares who wins, whether he picks winners, while acknowledging the fact that he cares about everyone and everything. I'm sure many fans have prayed for victory for their teams, but whether God takes these prayers under advisement, well, only he knows.

On occasion we might be left to wonder. On October 15, 1988, I was in South Bend, Indiana, to cover the Notre Dame-Miami football game for the *Orange County Register*. At the time, Notre Dame was 5-0 and fourth in the Associated Press ranking of college football teams, while Miami was 4-0 and ranked first. A pair of enterprising

Notre Dame students, Joe Frederick and Michael Caponigro, came up with an idea to sell T-shirts on which "Catholics vs. Convicts" was printed. Decades before social media, the slogan went viral in the run-up to the game, adding an interest-boosting Christian element of Good vs. Evil to what already was a highly anticipated game. The Catholics, of course, were represented by Notre Dame, the most prominent Catholic university in the country. Miami had the Convicts, who were so tagged as a result of several of its players having been arrested in the off-season.

Good vs. Evil, as themes go, who could resist?

This time, Good prevailed. Notre Dame won, 31–30, after Miami scored a touchdown with forty-five seconds left in the game, and rather than kicking an extra point to tie the game, they opted for a two-point conversion attempt for the win. A pass by Miami quarterback Steve Walsh was batted down and incomplete.

Divine intervention? Who knows, though I'll side with unlikely. Sports history is littered with scoundrels who won championships. Mike Tyson, for instance, was found guilty of rape in 1991 and was sentenced to six years in prison. He served fewer than two years, returned to boxing, and won the World Boxing Council heavyweight championship in 1996.

Some of sports' biggest stars—Pete Rose, Tiger Woods, John Daly, Kobe Bryant, Lawrence Taylor, Magic Johnson, and Mickey Mantle, among so many others—behaved in various ways that tarnished their reputations, temporarily, at least, yet all were exceptionally successful. We're all sinners in need of forgiveness.

Conversely, there were those faithful Christians who encountered the worst that could possibly happen in sports, and yet were able to rely on their faith to cope with the aftermath. Meet former Brooklyn Dodgers pitcher Ralph Branca. In 1951, in a one-game playoff with the New York Giants for the National League pennant, Branca gave up a game-winning, pennant-winning home run to Bobby Thomson in the bottom of the ninth, what quickly came to be known as the Shot Heard 'Round the World.

An unbylined post on the website ThroneberryFields.com

recounted the built-in ignominious reaction to failure in the white-hot cauldron of New York City sports and how Branca handled it.

"Too many Brooklyn fans thought Ralph Branca was on the wrong side of morality when he surrendered the maybe-it-is-/maybe-it-isn't tainted Shot Heard Round the World ending the 1951 National League pennant playoff. Branca's own priest thought otherwise and got to him fast enough. The priest told Branca God chose him because He knew he'd be strong enough to bear the burden. Branca proved stronger than those who wanted him drawn, quartered, and hung in the public square."

From personal experience, I can confirm that Branca lived his life largely unaffected by a single errant pitch. I was acquainted with Branca from spring training at Dodgertown in Vero Beach, Florida, in 1979. The Dodgers' staff—coaches, scouts, even manager Tommy Lasorda—played an annual game against the media. I was the media's catcher, and we had no one to pitch for us, so Branca took the mound on our behalf. My interactions with him, on and off the field that spring, convinced me that he was entirely unfazed by an experience that might have broken a lesser man. He was a delight to have gotten to know, and a reminder, from Romans 8:31, that "if God is for us, who can be against us?"

Yet the question that endures via a mainstream media that only charitably can be called secular rather than hostile to Christianity is whether God is a puppeteer, pulling the strings on sporting events. On two occasions over the years, *Sports Illustrated* asked the identical question, "Does God Care Who Wins the Super Bowl?" The first was from its January 26, 1998, edition. The full headline read: "DOES GOD CARE WHO WINS THE SUPER BOWL? MANY PACKERS AND BRONCOS THINK THE LORD WILL DECIDE THE OUTCOME. THEOLOGIANS BEG TO DIFFER."

The second time, in its February 4, 2013 edition, it was the cover story, featuring a photo of Ray Lewis of the Baltimore Ravens in a body of water with his hands together as though in prayer, with the simple headline, "Does God Care Who Wins the SUPER BOWL?"

Meanwhile, several years ago, a CNN story headlined "When did

God become a sports fan?" addressed the issue, with only a modicum of snark. "Thanking God from the winner's circle has become so common that one British newspaper published a letter to the editor entitled: 'Leave me out of your petty games—Love, God.' The British letter raised a question: Does God care who wins on game day? And, if so, do losers somehow have less faith?"

Again, I am just a layman intrigued by the question: Does God pick winners? Out of curiosity of what their answers might be, I posed the question to several Christian friends, including pastors, and the consensus was an emphatic no. Even NFL Hall of Fame quarterback Peyton Manning is an emphatic no. "Ah, but do I pray for victory?" he wrote in the book *Manning*, co-authored with his father Archie Manning. "No, except as a generic thing. I pray to keep both teams injury free, and personally that I use whatever talent I have to the best of my ability. But I don't think God really cares about who wins football games, except as winning might influence the character of some person or group."

But back to the Catholics versus the Convicts. I was staying in Chicago, and after writing my game story and on the drive from South Bend back to Chicago, the rental car radio was tuned to the first game of the World Series, the Dodgers versus the Oakland A's, at Dodger Stadium. I was somewhere on westbound Interstate 90 when an injured Kirk Gibson, a hamstring-pull in one leg, a knee injury in the other, was sent up to pinch hit in the bottom of the ninth inning with the Dodgers trailing, 4-3, and a runner on base. Gibson limped to the plate, as the partisan crowd roared its approval. On a full count, against all odds, well, here is the call from broadcasting legend Jack Buck:

We have a big three-two pitch coming here from [Dennis] Eckersley. Gibson swings, and a fly ball to deep right field. This is going to be a home run! Unbelievable! A home run for Gibson! And the Dodgers have won the game, five to four. I don't believe what I just saw!

I don't believe what I just saw! Is this really happening?

Meanwhile, the great Dodgers' broadcaster Vin Scully, a man I was privileged to have known from my days on the Dodgers' beat, memorably said in his own radio call, "In a year that has been so improbable, the impossible has happened!"

The Dodgers, behind pitcher Orel Hershiser, would go on to win the Series in five games. Hershiser, a Christian, was named the most valuable player of the Series, based on his two wins, including a complete-game victory to cinch it for the Dodgers in game five. During the fifth game, he appeared to be mouthing something to himself as he sat on the Dodgers' bench when his teammates were at bat, though in the post-game euphoria no one had asked him about it.

A day later, Hershiser was invited to appear on *The Tonight Show* with Johnny Carson. Hershiser is comfortable on a public stage, hence a second career in broadcasting, with ESPN and the Dodgers. Yet when Carson queried Hershiser on what he was saying to himself on the bench, Hershiser acknowledged that he was singing. Carson asked him to sing a few bars of whatever it was he was singing.

"No way I'm singing," Hershiser sheepishly replied.

"Yes, you are," Carson said, with the boisterous crowd urging Hershiser on. So he complied. He sang the popular Christian hymn, the Doxology:

> Praise God, from whom all blessings flow;
> Praise Him, all creatures here below;
> Praise Him above, ye heavenly host;
> Praise Father, Son, and Holy Ghost.
> Amen.

"That's very sweet," Carson said.

Was divine intervention at play on behalf of the Dodgers, with a devoutly Christian pitcher largely responsible for their winning the World Series? Probably not. I doubt that any serious Christian ever prays for victory or that they expect God to come down on the side of good vs. evil in sporting events. If outcomes were preordained from above, what would be the point?

Still, the subject has been revisited time and again over the years. A friend, Chris Dufresne of the *Los Angeles Times*, once wrote an in-depth story headlined, "Does God Care Who Wins," that ran more than 4,000 words. It was balanced and well-written and seasoned with Dufresne's entertaining wit, a combination that made him an accomplished sports journalist.

For instance, Dufresne wrote this regarding an NFL game between the Minnesota Vikings and the Detroit Lions: "And while league officials don't keep head counts, the number of religious athletes appears to be rising faster than a Roger Clemens fastball. Keith Johnson, the Minnesota Vikings' team chaplain, estimates 30 to 40 [Vikings] players regularly attend chapel services. Meaning, when Minnesota played at Detroit this season, it nearly was the Christians versus the Lions."

Well said, old friend.

More important were his theories for "the sudden stampede [of Christian athletes] into our living rooms." Here are two:

- Media exposure: Thirty years ago, religious athletes did not have the forum they have today. The explosion of television and cable channels has given players unprecedented access. "Everyone is looking for an angle, and more microphones are getting put in front of players," Price said. "Players are often getting the chance to talk in ways they were not given thirty years ago."
- The grass-roots movement worked: Youth-based religious groups formed in the fifties and sixties—Fellowship of Christian Athletes, Athletes in Action—have effectively permeated the sporting masses. In 1956, only 256 athletes and coaches attended the first Fellowship of Christian Athletes camp. In 1995, there were 13,048 participants. It

follows that many of those ministered to as youths would
carry their faith into the professional ranks.

I am not familiar with Chris's religious leanings, though with his
sad premature passing in 2020 at the age of sixty-two I hope that he
was right with the Lord. But the aforementioned bullet points are so
vitally important, more so twenty-three years after Dufresne wrote
them. Sports-oriented religious groups are living proof that the Holy
Spirit is at work. The forum that Christian athletes have, far greater
now than when Chris wrote this story, given that the Internet was still
in its formative years and social media did not exist, is vitally important in embracing the Great Commission.

Dufresne concluded his story noting that "some theologians"
thought the rise in Christian athletes expressing their faith was a fad
to which the Packers' Reggie White, the renowned "Minister of
Defense," took exception. A national newspaper advertising
campaign in 1999 urging White to stay the course on his public
proclamations of faith, had 175 current and former players signing
on in support.

"So get ready, America," the ad read in part, "because we're
standing with Reggie to defend the Gospel."

Still, the question is a recurring one—does God care who wins?
Or, as *Religion News Service* posed the question in advance of the
2017 Super Bowl between the Atlanta Falcons and New England
Patriots, "Does God give a holy hoot about the Super Bowl?"

The story was referring to a survey question by the Public Religion Research Institute, which produced interesting responses that
are somewhat conflicted. Forty-nine percent of all Americans polled,
it noted, agreed that "God rewards athletes who have faith with good
health and success," though only twenty-five percent agreed that
"God plays a role in determining which team wins a sporting event."

"Americans overall seem to hold what might be called a 'Provi-
dence Light' theology when it comes to sports," Robert P. Jones, the
CEO of Public Religion Research Institute, said. "While half of
Americans believe God may function as a kind of performance

enhancer for religious athletes, only one-quarter believe God actually throws the game to one side or the other."

The same poll showed that 26 percent of sports fans have "prayed for God to help their team." Twenty-five percent of them "believe their team is cursed."

A year earlier, LifeWay Research conducted a poll on whether God helps determine the Super Bowl winner. Of a thousand polled, 85 percent said no. "Our previous research has shown most Americans think God is concerned with their day-to-day decisions," said Scott McConnell, vice president of LifeWay Research. "Yet this survey shows Americans do not see God as interested in their favorite sport."

Bob Smietana, writing on the poll for LifeWay Research in advance of Super Bowl L between the Carolina Panthers and Denver Broncos, began his story this way: "An old gospel hymn says God's eye is on the sparrow, but what about panthers and broncos?"

I would argue, as did one of those I consulted, that God is interested in everything and everyone, though not in micromanaging sporting events. But he might use what transpired and those involved in ways that further the ultimate goal, to bring others to Christ.

The great quarterback Fran Tarkenton, a member of the Pro Football Hall of Fame, was what commonly is called a PK, a Preacher's Kid. In 2012, he wrote a story for the *Wall Street Journal*, its headline "Does God Care Who Wins Football Games?" In his piece, he notes that he "grew up the son of a Pentecostal Holiness minister – we were charismatic before charismatic was cool. I was in church Wednesday night, Friday night, Sunday morning and Sunday night – every week of my childhood."

Tarkenton recalled that in his playing days he questioned "why God would care who won a game between my team and another. It seemed like there were many far more important things going on in the world. There were religious guys on both teams. If God gets credit for the win, does he also take blame for the defeat?"

He confessed to having prayed "fervently" before each of the three Super Bowls he played in with the Minnesota Vikings. They lost all three, the last of them to the Oakland Raiders, "the villains of the league," he wrote, "and it was hard to believe they had more Christians on their team than on our saintly Vikings. We lost."

As Peyton Manning wrote in his book, "If the Colts were playing the Cowboys and I prayed for the Colts and Troy Aikman prayed for the Cowboys, wouldn't that make it a standoff?"

EIGHT

Mickey Mantle Goes to Heaven

MICKEY MANTLE often was described as larger than life, earning the distinction by squeezing everything he could from the immortality consigned him by having worn the pinstripes of the New York Yankees heroically while also burnishing his legend after hours in the town that never sleeps. He was sixty-three when he succumbed to liver cancer, thought to have been the consequence of his decades of waiting for last calls that never came.

I still go back and reread the Mantle obituary in *Sports Illustrated* written by my exceedingly talented long-time friend, Richard Hoffer. It is the best obituary of a renowned athlete I've ever read. It expertly captured how this son of an Oklahoma lead miner "was delivered from a rural obscurity into America's distilled essence of glamour," Hoffer wrote. "One year Mantle is dropping 400 feet into the earth, very deep into Oklahoma, to mine lead on his father's crew, another he's spilling drinks with Whitey Ford and Billy Martin at the Copa."

Hoffer's first paragraph of the obit:

Mickey Mantle, with his death Sunday at 63, passes from these pages forever and becomes the property of anthropologists, people who can more properly put the calipers to

celebrity, who can more accurately track the force of person-
ality. We can't do it anymore, couldn't really do it to begin
with. He batted this, hit that. You can look it up. Hell, we do
all the time. But there's nothing in our library, in all those
numbers, that explains how Mantle moves so smoothly from
baseball history into national legend, a country's touchstone,
the lopsided grin on our society.[1]

Mantle conquered the game, this perennial All-Star and first-
ballot Hall of Famer, and he did so in the cauldron of a city with fans
who have no tolerance for failure. But he could not conquer the
demons that eventually scripted an unhappy ending to a life lived
large.

Yet on closer inspection, was the ending all that unhappy,
notwithstanding its premature end that Mantle would have preferred
postponing given a choice?

Mantle was gifted in so many ways, but the most important was
that he was gifted with a remarkable Christian friend, his Yankees
teammate Bobby Richardson. They were not in the same league, if
talent was the only metric, though both were perennial all-stars.
Richardson was the antithesis of Mantle in every regard. He was a
singles hitter, his thirty-four career home runs only 502 fewer than
Mantle hit. He was a teetotaler, as well as a devout Christian, the
wholesome counter to teammates Mickey, Whitey, and Billy, "just
boys, really, they all had little boys' names," Hoffer wrote. Bobby is
a little boy's name, too, but he was the adult in the room.

Richardson and Mantle were friends and the strangest of bedfellows. As we have come to learn over the years, the Holy Spirit was
working on Mantle through Richardson.

I had heard some of the story of Richardson's influence on
Mantle, notably when the latter was approaching death. But I was
interested in hearing it from Richardson himself. I knew he lived in
Sumter, South Carolina, as he had his entire life, and I found an
address for him, but no phone number or email address. So on
February 24, 2022, I sent him a letter, briefly explaining my back-

ground and interest in talking with him about the intersection of Christianity and sports. I concluded the letter with this:

> I would like to speak with you for 20 minutes or so to get your thoughts, as a devout Christian and former MLB player whose impact on others, notably Mickey Mantle, still resonate with Christians today.
>
> Please let me know your availability. And God bless.

I had not expected to hear back from him, frankly. He was eighty-seven at the time, but three weeks later to the day, my phone rang, and it showed that the call was emanating from Sumter, South Carolina, Richardson's hometown.

The ensuing forty or so minutes were among the most enjoyable I've spent talking to a former athlete, in this case a man who was part of one of sports' greatest dynasties, the New York Yankees in the fifties and sixties, and a Christian man who lived his faith openly, an unspoken invitation to those searching for answers to difficult questions about this life and the next to seek his counsel. Eventually, Mantle RSVP'd to that invitation.

"Let me just say this," Richardson said at the outset of our conversation. "What a great teammate he was. His whole career, there when I got there and when I left."

Richardson's faith informs him, and he was aware that the Holy Spirit was working through him with Mantle, among others. "It really started," Richardson said, "when Roger Maris at fifty-one went on to be with the Lord."

Richardson gave the eulogy at the funeral for Maris, best known for hitting sixty-one home runs to eclipse Babe Ruth's record of sixty set thirty-four years earlier. Maris's funeral service was at St. Mary's Cathedral in his hometown of Fargo, North Dakota. The pallbearers included teammates Mantle, Ford, Moose Skowron, and Whitey Herzog.

"At Roger's funeral," Richardson said, "Mickey sat down beside me and said, 'I want you to have my funeral.' When I would see him again, it was the same, every time."

Richardson recalled a conversation he had had with Mantle when they were together in Phoenix for three days for a Make-A-Wish Foundation function. "He'd been drinking a little bit," Richardson said. "He said, 'When I was growing up, I attended church Sunday morning and Sunday night. But when I got to New York, I got away from it.'

"I realized he had a genuine love [for the Lord] and a background, so when I talked to him about the Lord, I talked to him in a tactful way."

Richardson said there were not many Christians on the Yankees teams in those days, or at least Christians of whom he was aware. His keystone partner, shortstop Tony Kubek, was one of them, and together they were dubbed the Milkshake Twins. Richardson always invited Mantle to join Kubek and him for Sunday morning services on road trips.

Richardson did not force his faith on others, while also noting that "I don't think I gave them the occasion to react in the wrong way. I remember we had beer in the clubhouse. My oldest son Rich was about five at the time." Richardson said that one day after a game that one of the players said, "Hey, Rich, come over and have a beer so you can grow up like me."

Richardson politely told the player that he would appreciate him not doing that. "He later apologized to me about fifteen times," Richardson said.

He lived his faith openly, though without proselytizing, allowing the Holy Spirit to work through him. He became the go-to man for delivering eulogies for Christian baseball players having passed away. "The first one was Maris," he said. "They asked me to represent the ballclub and to give the eulogy. [Pitcher] Bob Turley's son asked me. [Hall of Fame outfielder] Enos Slaughter's daughter, she asked me to have her dad's funeral. I was part of twelve teammates' funerals."

When Mantle's health was failing and he was nearing the end,

Richardson was summoned from South Carolina to Dallas by Mantle's friend and lawyer Roy True. When he entered the hospital room, Richardson was determined once again to express the importance of faith because, as he had said on more than once occasion, that he wanted Mickey "to spend eternity with me in heaven."

This is the essence of the Great Commission, the end goal to Matthew 28:19, to "make disciples of all nations," to bring others to Christ.

Mantle died shortly after that and Richardson eulogized his friend, per Mick's request many years earlier. This is from his eulogy:

> Roy True said, "Mickey's not doing very well and the family would like for you to consider the possibility of coming out and being in the service." And I asked Merlyn [Mantle's wife] if it would be alright if I could come on out and she said "yes." Well, I came in on, I guess it was last Wednesday night. Friends picked me up at the airport and I spent the night with them, it was late. And the next morning, I drove over to Baylor Hospital. Whitey Ford was just walking out at the time and Mickey had really perked up with Whitey's visit. And as I walked in and went over to his bed, he had that smile on his face. And he looked at me and the first thing he said was, "Bobby, I've been wanting to tell you something. I want you to know that I've received Christ as my savior." Well, I cried a little bit, I'm sure, and we had prayer together and then in a very simple way I said, "Mickey, I just want to make sure," and I went over God's plan of salvation with him. That God loved us and had a plan, a purpose and a plan for all of us and sent his son, the Lord Jesus Christ, to shed his precious blood and promise in his word that if we repent of our sins and receive the Lord Jesus that we might not only have everlasting life but the joy of letting him live his life in us. He said, "That's what I've done."

Later that same day, Richardson said he and his wife Betsy returned to see Mantle. Again, from Richardson's eulogy:

Betsy sat down by him and shared her testimony. And then she asked him a question. She said, "Mickey, if God were here today and you were standing before him and he would ask the question, Why should I let you in my heaven, what would you say?" And as quick as a flash, he said, "For God so loved the world he gave his only begotten son and whosoever believeth in him should not parish but have everlasting life."

John 3:16, "the heart of the Bible" and "the heart of the gospel," as the verse has been called.

Everyone should have a Bobby Richardson in their life, a Christian determined to lead friends to faith by using the tools that Christ has given us, notably the Holy Spirit, and to "want to spend eternity in heaven" with your friends. What a remarkably heartwarming thought.

"The big thing is to be tactful," he told me. "Let the Lord and the Holy Spirit empower you."

When Richardson was nearing retirement, the Yankees held a Bobby Richardson Day at Yankee Stadium, September 17, 1966, the tenth day held for a Yankee player, the most memorable having been Lou Gehrig Day, when Gehrig, dying of amyotrophic lateral sclerosis, ALS, famously declared, "Today I consider myself the luckiest man on the face of the earth."

In advance of his own day, Richardson was told, "We don't want to make this a church service." Richardson suggested instead that he write a gospel tract to be handed out to all the fans, which he did, funding it himself. The legendary gospel singer George Beverly Shea, a frequent soloist on the Billy Graham Crusades, sang "How Great Thou Art."

"I was very tactful," Richardson said. "Athletes can have tremendous influence, but they have to be careful. I saw the film *Pride of the Yankees* when I was young." He noted Gehrig's famous quote, and wanted something as impactful, without duplicating it. He concluded his speech with this:

> As I think of baseball and the memories I've had in the past
> ten-and-a-half years, I think of the opportunities. And in
> closing I can only say as Mickey Mantle has said, as Lou
> Gehrig has said, how lucky it has been for me to have been a
> Yankee. To God be the glory. Thank you very much.

It was a perfect sendoff, save for one minor detail pointed out by Richardson's mother-in-law. "We are not lucky," she said, "we are blessed."

Mothers, or in this case mothers-in-law, know best.

In Richardson's hometown of Sumter, there is a Bobby Richardson Baseball Complex that features baseball bollards, large baseballs made of glass fiber and reinforced concrete, on top of pedestals. Two of them feature Richardson's favorite Bible verses:

> For I delivered to you as of first importance what I also
> received: that Christ died for our sins in accordance with the
> Scriptures, that he was buried, that he was raised on the third
> day in accordance with the Scriptures. (1 Corinthians 15:3–4)

> For I am not ashamed of the gospel, because it is the power
> of God that brings salvation to everyone who believes: first to
> the Jew, then to the Gentile. (Romans 1:16)

Again, everyone should have a Bobby Richardson in their life, dedicated, as he was to Mickey, to ensuring that they spend eternity in heaven together. What a beautiful sentiment. To God be the glory, indeed.

NINE

Separation of Church and. . . Sports?

IT IS NOT a revelation that most in the mainstream media on the news side lean so far left they are in danger of tipping over. What might be revelatory, however, is that many of those in sports media do, too, and they are not shy about demonstrating their bias whenever the opportunity presents itself. Recall that the media was far more amenable to Colin Kaepernick kneeling in protest than it was for Tim Tebow kneeling in prayer.

Generally, the media does not view Christianity favorably. Hugh Hewitt is a long-time talk radio show host, a law professor, a former assistant White House counsel in the Reagan administration, a Christian, a *Washington Post* columnist, and a brilliant man for whom I have the greatest admiration. (A disclosure is necessary here: Hugh wrote a blurb for my previous book, *A Snowflake Named Hannah: Ethics, Faith, and the First Adoption of a Frozen Embryo.*) He is one of the most astute observers of life in America, politically and culturally. He was interviewed by the estimable Dr. James Dobson, a family friend of ours and the founder of Focus on the Family, and said this about the media: "The elite media in this country has great contempt for Christianity. In almost every newspaper, in almost every network, in almost every elite magazine that I have become familiar, and I'm a journalist, so I read all of these, there is an under-lying tenor of not just disrespect, but contempt for people who believe that Christ is God and does save from sins."

I agree, and it bleeds into the sports media, probably to its detri-ment. In 2013, the Barna Group, a leading research organization focused on the intersection of faith and culture, conducted a study on "the influence of athletes and the role faith plays in American sports." The study suggests rather strongly that the media is on the wrong side of this issue. Sixty-one percent of adults polled "say they favor professional and prominent college athletes talking about their faith in media or events seen by the general public." Only 12 percent were opposed. It also asked about specific Christian athletes, including Tim Tebow. It noted that 83 percent of Americans are aware of Tebow and that 73 percent feel favorably about his public discussion of faith. The numbers for Clayton Kershaw were 25 percent on awareness and 78 percent on favorability of his public discussion of faith. Dave Kinnaman, the CEO of the Barma Group, said, "That there's such a strong and positive awareness of Tim Tebow and his faith reveals Americans—and particularly Christians —desire for an authentic role model who is willing to so publicly connect his faith and life."

In press boxes and media centers around the country, and in the news rooms in which I have worked, I was always an outlier—a pro-life Christian conservative. I was not alone, but our numbers gener-ally were so small that we tended to temper our opinions. The other side was not similarly guarded in expressing their opinions. My conclusion from decades of moving in these circles was that most of those in press boxes, media centers, and newsrooms just assumed everyone there thought as they did. For the most part, they were right.

In 1994, I was working for the *Orange County Register*, at the time an enormously successful newspaper, among the best in the country. That was the year that Congressman Newt Gingrich and his Contract with America resulted in both the House of Representatives and the Senate flipping from Democrats to Republicans. The

Register incidentally was part of a newspaper group owned by a family that leaned heavily libertarian. The newsroom, nonetheless, leaned in an opposite direction. In the wake of the Republican takeover, a post on a newsroom bulletin board was an invitation to a party to mourn the Contract with America victory. Virtually no one in the newsroom, editors or reporters, found this objectionable, at a newspaper with libertarian ownership.

Again, I was part of a small minority, even among my colleagues in the sports department. Over the years I came to agree with those advancing the notion that sportswriters have an inferiority complex from working in what often has been described as the toy department. We write about games. So when opportunities presented themselves to pontificate in print on more serious matters, sports columnists tended to embrace them, meanwhile openly objecting to public displays of Christianity, knowing no opposition is forthcoming from editors. Maybe I'm wrong, but this has been my experience.

Generally they were in safe spaces when they opposed Christian athletes expressing their faith, knowing they had the support of so many others in the media—friends, colleagues, and even editors. Objections were few, if any. As Mark Twain famously said about the media in general, "Never pick an argument with people who buy ink by the barrel."

This was evident to me even among the golf media. Rough estimates of PGA Tour players in the past suggested that upwards of 90 percent of them were Republican, many of them Christians, too. Yet the percentage of those reporting on them was substantially lower.

Christians are called to defend their faith, as I've previously noted, and Scripture supports: "But in your hearts honor Christ the Lord as holy, always being prepared to make a defense to anyone who asks you for a reason for the hope that is in you; yet do it with gentleness and respect" (1 Peter 3:15 ESV). And as the great atheist turned renowned theologian, C.S. Lewis, once said, "We must show our Christian colors if we are to be true to Jesus Christ."

When I was covering sports for newspapers, including many

night games that finished on, near, or even after deadline, I confess that I was among the writers with pressing deadlines rolling their eyes when a Christian athlete in a post-round interview began by thanking their Lord and Savior before answering questions. I am not proud of that fact, but again, I am a sinner and deadlines were looming.

The anti-Christian bias from the sports media, or at least its opposition to expressions of faith, reliably resurfaces in a timely fashion every year, as it did in the case of former NFL coach Tony Dungy, now an NBC Sports analyst, in early 2023. I have never met him, but I know those who do know him, and the consensus is that he is a world-class man guided by his Christian faith and wholly undeterred by criticism of it.

Dungy was blistered by the media in the aftermath of his having posted what was considered an anti-trans tweet for which he quickly and profusely apologized. "I saw a tweet yesterday and I responded to it in the wrong way. As a Christian I should speak in love and in ways that are caring and helpful. I failed to do that and I am deeply sorry."

Dungy's faith, firmly rooted in the Bible, informs all he does in response to his sins. "Whoever conceals his transgressions will not prosper, but he who confesses and forsakes them will obtain mercy" (Proverbs 28:13 ESV).

The antidote to the media's inherent bias against Christians in sports it to disregard it, as Dungy does well. Don't dwell on it, and remember Paul's words: "If God is for us, who can be against us?" (Romans 8:31 ESV). The animosity, even hatred, is a given, and has been for decades, toward those who don't keep their faith to themselves.

Nothing will quell the mainstream media's aversion to public displays of affection for Jesus Christ. It is not new, either. Frank Deford was a brilliant writer at *Sports Illustrated* in the decades that the magazine was a must-read for sports fans with an interest in literary storytelling. In 1976, Deford authored a three-part series, "Religion in Sport." It was not particularly flattering to Christians.

The series ran to nearly 16,000 words, all of them carefully chosen and meshing expertly as one would expect from an exceptionally gifted wordsmith. Of course, gifted wordsmiths can do snark better than anyone.

Deford combined sports and Christians to form two new words —*sportians* and *sportianity*. He wrote in his first installment:

Jocks for Jesus is booming. It is almost as if a new denomination had been created: Sportianity. While Christian churches struggle with problems of declining attendance, falling contributions and now even reduction in membership, Sportianity appears to be taking off. . .

Jesus has been transformed, emerging anew as a holler guy, a hustler, a give-it-100-percenter. While students of the new religion glumly acknowledge that his only known athletic performance was throwing the moneychangers out of the temple, Jesus' sad, desperate last hours have become a kind of Super Bowl.

And this from Deford's second installment:

Increasingly, public team prayer and public-address entreaties to the Divine Goalie or the Head Coach in the Sky are in evidence. Sportianity, as this brand of religion might best be called, is thoroughly evangelistic, using sport as an advertising medium. The idea is simple enough: first, convert the athletes, who are among the most visible individuals in our society; then, use these stars for what is generally known in the business as "outreach," an up-to-date rendering of the old-fashioned phrase "missionary work." To put it bluntly, athletes are being used to sell religion. They endorse Jesus, much as they would a new sneaker or a graphite-shafted driver.

And this from the third installment, in summary:

> In the final analysis, sport has had a greater impact upon religion than the other way around. While athletics does not appear to have been improved by the religious blitzkrieg, the religious people who work that side of the street seem to have been colored by some of the worst attitudes found in sport. . . It might be a good idea right now to talk to the veteran GM in the sky about the possibility of a rebuilding year.[1]

I concede that Deford was far smarter than I am, given his Princeton degree, but how could he not know that "outreach" and "missionary work" is what Christians are called to do, according to the Great Commission? I have read that Deford was a man of faith, "a layperson chosen to read scripture from the pulpit at Christ & Holy Trinity Episcopal Church in Westport, Conn.," wrote Terry Mattingly at GetReligion.org, citing a Westport publication's obituary of Deford.

I sincerely hope he was a Christian, of course, but his objections to Christianity effectively having found a voice in sports aligned neatly with the mainstream media at large, coming down on the side of keeping them separated, á la church and state. His series of stories, the execution of which was exceptional, was indicative of the disdain the sports media have demonstrated over the years toward Christian athletes and their mentors who take seriously the Great Commission, to "go and make disciples of all nations, baptizing them in the name of the Father and of the Son and of the Holy Spirit," as it says in the book of Matthew. Mark also wrote about it: "And he said to them, 'Go into all the world and proclaim the gospel to the whole creation'" (Mark 16:15 ESV).

There is no equivocation in those passages; they do not suggest in any manner that those who have the public's attention might want to refrain from utilizing the fact that they have an audience to proclaim God's word. The message in those verses is clear: Proclaim the gospel and let the Holy Spirit take over.

It pains me, as a career sportswriter, how often the sports media use their platforms to mock, if not to outright condemn, Christianity when it surfaces in sports. My file on sports media criticism of Christian athletes is by a wide margin the most extensive of all my research files.

The most recent example of the media's bias came in the aftermath of the Philadelphia Flyers' Ivan Provorov declining to join teammates wearing a gay pride-themed pregame jersey on the team's annual Pride Night celebration. He cited his religion, Russian Orthodox, to explain why he declined to participate.

"I respect everybody's choices," Provorov told reporters after the game. "My choice is to stay true to myself and my religion. That's all I'm going to say."

Provorov was excoriated by the media. NHL Network's E. J. Hradek suggested that putting him in an imaginary penalty box wasn't nearly severe enough punishment. "If this is that much of a problem for him to maybe assimilate into his group of teammates and in the community and here in this country, that's okay," Hradek wrote. "Listen, you can feel any way you want, but the beauty is, if it bothers you that much, there's always a chance to leave. Go back where you feel more comfortable. I understand there's a conflict going on over there. Maybe get involved."

Hradek was referring to the Russia-Ukraine "conflict."

A hockey writer for *Sports Illustrated* and the *Hockey News* tweeted this: "The Flyers, like every team in the NHL, have LGBTQ+ identifying fans. Ivan Provorov just told them all that he doesn't think they belong in hockey. Disgusting."

Provorov told them no such thing, of course, but he had ventured into territory the media declares should be off limits.

The only apparent "hate" in this affair came from those in the sports media with disdain for Christian athletes following their faith. They do so without fear of recrimination because they are part of an overwhelming majority in their profession.

The National Hockey League to its credit released a statement on behalf of its players supporting causes important to them. "Clubs decide whom to celebrate, when and how—with League counsel and support," the statement read in part. "Players are free to decide which initiatives to support, and we continue to encourage their voices and perspectives on social and cultural issues."

John Stonestreet, the president of the Colson Center for Christian Worldview and a friend, was the voice of reason on this so-called controversy, with this statement:

> You Can Play, a social activism group associated with the NHL's "hockey is for everyone" campaign, offered to re-educate Provorov, and COO Kurt Weaver publicly questioned whether he should even be a member of the team if he disagrees on issues of LGBTQ. "At what point does a decision like this that a player wants to make cross over into basically not showing up for your job?" asked Weaver.

> So, that's the job of a hockey player now? You Can Play says hockey is for everyone, but they don't really mean it. They are among the many pundits who preach diversity and practice conformity. Thankfully, the NHL stated that it will continue to "celebrate the diversity" and "players are free to decide which initiatives to support."

> That's actual diversity.

The groupthink in sports media's general aversion to Christianity nonetheless remains prevalent.

Rick Reilly is an exceptionally talented sportswriter, who I have known probably since 1981 or 1982. I've played basketball, softball, and golf with him. I've hoisted beers with him. When I was working for the *Orange County Register*, Reilly was hired by the *Los Angeles Times*'s Orange County Edition. His talent was immediately evident, and eventually *Sports Illustrated* hired him. The feature stories he wrote for that magazine were extraordinary, two of which stand out for me to this day—his 1986 profile of legendary *Los Angeles Times* columnist Jim Murray and his 1988 profile of Bryant Gumbel, head-lined, "The Mourning Anchor." The latter was among the *SI 60 Series*, sixty of the magazine's best stories identified on the sixtieth anniversary of the magazine.

His Murray profile began this way: "The thing about Jim Murray is that he lived 'happily,' but somebody ran off with his 'ever after.'" Brilliant. Murray lost a son to drugs, a wife to cancer, and his eyesight for a few years. Murray was not only the best sports colum-nist in the country, in the opinion of many, including me, but he also was the nicest and most gracious, except, I note facetiously, in a golf press center, when he was sitting next to me. After he would finish another great column in relatively quick fashion, he would turn to me grinding away on my story, and say, "It doesn't have to rhyme." He had a sharp needle at his disposal that he always used in jest. I first became acquainted with him in 1970, when I was a college freshman and went to work for the *Los Angeles Times*. He became a great friend, and to this day his wife Linda Murray Hofmans (she eventually remarried after Murray's death in 1998) remains a good friend.

I note all of this because I respect Reilly, but he, too, joined the media's anti-Christianity choir with his February 4, 1991, column that carried this headline: "Save Your Prayers, Please: Organized Worship Has No Place at Football Games." The column began with this:

> Harry Truman once said that when you hear someone praying real loud, that is the time to lock up the smokehouse. Well, the praying was deafening during this NFL season.

Never mind that President Truman was only quoting what he had heard from his uncle, (though he said, "I think he was right from the little I have observed"). The column was a rebuttal to the post-game prayer circles that had begun in the NFL the season before. It mysti-fies me why anyone would care, much less object. Maybe it was a slow news week and Reilly was bereft of ideas. But for a man of his talent to suddenly turn his focus to an innocuous demonstration of Christian faith is inexplicable. Here is his second paragraph:

> It's the latest thing: Ringed by TV minicams, a dozen or so fervent Christian players from both teams join at midfield after game, drop to their knees, clasp hands, bow heads and pray. A stadium full of people and a national television audience are in attendance, whether they like it or not. You saw some New York Giants do it during the postseason, with a delegation of Chicago Bears. And you saw a group of Buffalo Bills do it with some Los Angeles Raiders after their AFC Championship Game.

Again, these prayer circles happen *after* the games, when fans are exiting the stadium and television doing its best to avoid showing them. Reilly never explained the harm it might have done, because there was none. Moreover, he wrote how Giants quarterback Jeff Hostetler, rather than joining the prayer circle, "ran to his locker, knelt in front of it and prayed. He was keeping it private." Well, at least until Reilly helped to publicize it.

I don't know what Reilly believes, but Christians understand God's command to spread his word and help bring others to faith. We aren't called to hide our faith in the event it might give some in the audience, or in the press box, the vapors.

I bring this up not to specifically single out an old friend, but to highlight how those in the sports media, many of whom might well be Christians, have a genuine disdain for athletes showing affection for Jesus.

It was a given that as the Black Lives Matter protests were embraced by athletes and supported by those in the sports media, that any dissent from the orthodoxy would be met with a torrent of media criticism, some of it vile. New Orleans Saints quarterback Drew Brees was the most prominent target for speaking out against those kneeling for the National Anthem. And to a lesser degree, San Francisco Giants pitcher Jeff Coonrod and Jonathan Isaac of the Orlando

Magic made their religious objections to kneeling in support of the Black Lives Matter movement.

Isaac was the first player in the NBA who declined to kneel. He, too, declined to wear a BLM T-shirt during the pre-game warm up.

The first question asked of him post-game, oddly, considering the fact that Isaac is African American: "Do you believe black lives matter?"

Isaac handled the question with aplomb. "Absolutely, I believe that black lives matter. A lot went into my decision. And part of it is first off, is my thought that kneeling or wearing a Black Lives Matter T-shirt don't go hand-in-hand with supporting black lives. . . I do believe that black lives matter, but I just felt like it was a decision that I had to make. And I didn't feel like putting that shirt on and kneeling went hand-in-hand with supporting black lives or that it made me support black lives. And I don't believe that.

"For myself, my life has been supported through the Gospel, Jesus Christ, and that everyone is made in the image of God and that we all fall short of God's glory and that each and every one of us, each and every day, do things that we shouldn't do. We say things that we shouldn't say. We hate and we dislike people that we shouldn't hate and dislike. And sometimes it gets into a point where we point fingers about whose evil is worse. And sometimes it comes out as simply whose evil is most visible.

"So I felt like I wanted to just take a stand on it. I feel like we all make mistakes. But I think the Gospel of Jesus Christ is that there's grace for us and that Jesus came and died for our sins and that we all will come to an understanding of that and understand that God wants to have a relationship with us, that we can get past skin color. We can get past all the things in our world that are messed up, jacked up.

"I think when you look around, racism isn't the only thing that plagues our society, that plagues our nation, that plagues our world. And I feel like coming together on that message that we want to get past not only racism but everything that plagues us as a society, I feel like the answer to it is the Gospel."

It was an intelligent, thoughtful answer in defense of his faith, yet to many in the media it was insufficient. Among them was Dan Le Batard, a talented former *Miami Herald* columnist, who moved on to ESPN with his own radio show. Isaac's religious stance occurred on a Friday and on Sunday he tore his anterior cruciate ligament. The next day, on *The Dan Le Batard Show,* Le Batard put out a poll with the question: "Is it funny the guy who refused to kneel immediately blew out his knee?"

The backlash was enough to cause Le Batard to issue an apology on Twitter: "We apologize for this poll question. I said on the front and back end of the on-air conversation that I didn't think it was funny. Regardless of the context, we missed the mark. We took the tweet down when we realized our mistake in how we posed the question to the audience. -Dan"

The apology did not play particularly well. Todd Jones, a Republican State House Representative in Georgia's District 25, responded on Twitter: "Reason 1,001 to keep sports and politics separate. Stop intertwining the two...I only want to hear your thoughts on first downs, OPS, golf handicaps and other sports related matters."

The examples of the sports media's anti-Christianity bias are not few. I will conclude with this, a quote I previously mentioned for its effectiveness in soundbite witnessing. The quote was from Texas A&M kicker Seth Small in the aftermath of his game-winning field goal against Alabama.

"It was probably the third best moment of my life," he said. "Right after I accepted Jesus into my heart as my true Lord and Savior, and then after getting married to my wife this summer, I'd rank this three."

It was a great quote that was not necessarily appreciated by all, to wit an obviously intentional omission in a story in *Sports Illustrated.* Our family friend, Paul Batura, vice president of communications for Focus on the Family and a man for whom I have the highest respect, writing for its *Daily Citizen* website, noted: "Acute readers of *Sports Illustrated,* the iconic sports magazine, might be left trying to piece together the kicker's full comments. In a piece published yesterday, SI's Andrew Gastelum writes:

After the game, Small said in his postgame press conference that the kick ranked as the "third best moment of my life"— right after marrying his wife over the summer."

"Gastelum leaves out Small's reference to Jesus – even though readers following along would inevitably wonder what the number one moment of the kicker's life would be."

How his editor could have read that and not concurred is a mystery, though a clue is the media's general disdain for Christianity, or at least public displays of it.

Incidentally, Small approached the game and the winning field goal by repeatedly reciting to himself: "The LORD is my shepherd; I shall not want" (Psalm 23:1 ESV).

"And that kind of comforted me," he said. "That's a moment I live for, and I just kind of want to focus on that and then celebrate with [teammates] afterward – just so I can deliver on my part, [because] they've been delivering on their part all night long."

I will let Batura have the last words, given that he said it so well.

"That *Sports Illustrated* would choose to write an article focused on the personal side of Small – and leave out the most important detail of the young man's personal life – is yet another reminder secular culture is increasingly uncomfortable with any reference to the Christian faith, especially evangelicalism.

"We'll never know if the prophet Isaiah would have been a football fan, but he was surely determined to set future football fans straight when he wrote, 'The grass withers, the flower fades, but the word of our God will stand forever [Isaiah 40:8].'

"Congratulations to Seth Small on Saturday's big win (and condolences to Alabama), but special kudos to a man who has his priorities of faith, family and football straight."

TEN

Remember the Sabbath to Keep It. . . What's that Again?

WHEN YOUR JOB, *your livelihood*, depends on your working on Sundays, it clashes with a biblical edict, to "Remember the Sabbath day, to keep it holy. Six days you shall labor, and do all your work, but the seventh day is a Sabbath to the LORD your God. On it you shall not do any work, you, or your son, or your daughter, your male servant, or your female servant, or your livestock, or the sojourner who is within your gates" (Exodus 20:8–10 ESV).

There is no caveat there, one that says "unless your team is playing," or "unless your boss has assigned you to cover a game or a tournament."

The Sabbath, as Christians regard it, is Sunday, the most important day of the week for the National Football League, but also important for all other professional sports that depend on large audiences for their wherewithal. Given that most people have weekends off from work, it is sound business to schedule games and tournaments on weekends. I am pointing out the obvious, of course, but regarding the Sabbath, Christian sports fans often find ways to accommodate both, by putting God first and the team second. Several years ago, we attended a church service in Aurora, Colorado, where the pastor, Tim Lawson, was a family friend. It happened to fall on a Sunday on which the Denver Broncos were playing, and several of the parishioners were wearing Broncos jerseys. Whether they were praying for a Broncos victory, well, that was between them and our Savior. But at least their priorities were in order—Jesus first, the Broncos second.

I fully understand the conflict, having spent virtually my entire adult life working on Sundays. Obviously, sportswriters, as do the athletes and teams on whom they report, work weekends. Major League Baseball, the NFL, and the PGA Tour, my three principal beats in my long career in sports journalism, schedule games and tournaments on weekends.

The Masters, one of the most important and widely viewed sports events on the calendar, always concludes on the second Sunday in April. And occasionally, those Sundays fall on Easter. The LPGA's first major championship of the season, the old Dinah Shore now known as the Chevron Championship, had always been played the week prior to the Masters, so it, too, occasionally would conclude on Easter Sunday. On those occasions, the LPGA, to its credit, would hold an Easter Sunrise Service for its players, their families, and the media, on the eighteenth green at Mission Hills Country Club in Rancho Mirage, California.

Suffice it to say that it would not have been a good career move to let the boss know that I was not going to work Sundays, Easter or otherwise.

Billy Graham, the legendary evangelist, a remarkable man, and an avid golfer and sports fan, nonetheless once considered Sunday sports to be anathema to God's edict in Exodus. He held this position even as late as 1955. "The world needs today people with conviction enough in things Christian to refuse to conform to the popular trend," he wrote then. "People with sufficient regard for the highest things to say, 'Not today, thank you,' when asked on the Lord's Day to turn from work to play rather than from work to worship."

A year earlier, UCLA's football team had gone 9-0 and won the national championship. The team was dubbed the Eleven from Heaven, "so-named because the majority of the starting lineup was involved with Campus Crusade for Christ, including a pair of star players—Donn Moomaw and Bob Davenport—who refused to play in the NFL after their college careers," Paul Putz wrote in a story for *Athletes in Action.* "For Moomaw and Davenport, playing football on Sunday was a sin that undermined their Christian witness."

Putz included in his article, headlined "How Billy Graham Made Peace With Sunday Sports," an amusing quote from an evangelist in the 1920s, Howard S. Williams, on his opposition to a professional football game scheduled for a Sunday in New Orleans. "There will not be a single Christian [in attendance]," Johnson said. "Probably, however, hundreds of church members will be there."

Ouch.

When Graham died in 2018, I was asked to write his obituary for GolfDigest.com, not that I was the only Christian on the staff. But I was perhaps the most visible Christian, via social media posts, and I do have Graham's autobiography, *Just as I Am,* on a shelf in my home office. Graham was a sports fan, who in his autobiography wrote, "Athletes like tennis star Michael Chang, professional golfers Gary Player and Bernhard Langer, and football coach Tom Landry have taken a stand for Christ. They and many others have become friends of mine over the years." Golf, I noted in the obituary, is mentioned on thirty-nine different pages in his book. Graham played in PGA Tour pro-ams, twice with President Gerald Ford and once with Bob Hope. In 2010, to commemorate *Golf Digest*'s sixtieth anniversary, the magazine did a feature headlined, "60 Most Famous Golfers." Billy Graham was among the sixty. His most famous quote about the game, an enduring one, was this: "The only time my prayers are never answered are on the golf course."

Graham eventually came around to acknowledging that it was acceptable for sports to be played on Sundays by Christian athletes, noting that times had changed, and on this one point that it was better for Christianity overall that it changed, too. Even Pope Francis was on board for Sunday games, provided they do not interfere with worship, according to a 2018 Vatican document titled, "Giving the Best of Yourself."

"The document. . . condoned sports on Sundays as a means of bringing families and communities together in joy and celebration," the *National Catholic Reporter* noted in its story, "but only as long as such events are not used as an excuse to miss Mass."

Santiago Perez de Camino, head of the Church and Sport Office for the Dicastery for the Laity, the Family, and Life, was quoted in the same *National Catholic Register* story, saying that Christian athletes provide "a very beautiful witness of how to join faith with sport."

However, there have been hardliners, those opposed to competing on the Sabbath, throughout history, and among the most prominent was the Scottish Olympic gold medalist Eric Liddell, the Flying Scotsman, a devout Christian and future missionary who steadfastly refused to compete on Sundays.

Liddell was one of the best sprinters in the world in 1924, and his best event was the 100 meters. But the 100-meter heats in the Olympic Games in Paris were scheduled for a Sunday, the Sabbath, so Liddell chose not to enter the event. Instead, he opted to run the 400 meters. He was not expected to win, nor even to medal, based on his 400 times in advance of the Olympics. Yet he won the gold medal and set a world record, 47.6 seconds, that became the impetus behind the film that made him famous nearly sixty years later.

Remembering the Sabbath to keep it holy has always been a challenge to Christian athletes required to play games on Sundays. When I spoke recently with Bobby Richardson, a star second baseman for the New York Yankees in the late fifties and early sixties, about his steadfast Christian faith, he recounted a particular Sunday in Minneapolis, when the Yankees were scheduled to play a doubleheader with the Minnesota Twins. Richardson and shortstop Tony Kubek first wanted to attend services at a church where Richardson knew the pastor. "Tony and I said, 'Hey, Mick, you want to go with us?'" Richardson told me. Mick, of course, was teammate Mickey Mantle, a legend on the field, but also off the field, the result of his renowned post-game proclivities that included running mates Billy Martin and Whitey Ford.

Mickey agreed to go with them to church. Richardson was concerned, though, that with Mantle in tow they probably would need to sneak out of the service a few minutes early to avoid the commotion Mickey's appearance would cause. They were concerned mostly that they would not make it to the ballpark in time for the start of batting practice. So upon arrival, Richardson explained to Mantle and Kubek that with about ten minutes before the end of the service, they'd have to sneak out to get to the ballpark on time for batting practice. He had arranged to have a taxi standing by and said that when it was apparent the preacher was nearing the end of his message, they'd quietly head for the exit.

It was a good idea in theory, but in practice?

When they stood to leave, many in the congregation recognized Mantle and mayhem predictably ensued, including a photo request from the pastor who said, "I want a picture with my son." The trio eventually missed batting practice.

When Red Barber, the Yankees' legendary broadcaster and a lay minister, heard the story, and once the laughter had subsided, he suggested that Christian players ought to have a Sunday Bible study in the clubhouse, eliminating the issue of finding a church and then after the service having to rush to get to the ballpark.

Those team chapels became a Sunday routine that was the fore-runner of the organization now known as Baseball Chapel.

Baseball Chapel is "an international ministry recognized by Major and Minor League Baseball and is responsible for the appointment and oversight of all team chapel leaders (over 500 throughout professional baseball)," its website states. "Baseball Chapel's ministry extends throughout Major and Minor League Baseball, and reaches outside the United States serving leagues in Mexico, Puerto Rico, Venezuela, the Dominican Republic, Nicaragua and Japan."

NFL teams also have chaplains, two of whom once conspired to bring greater attention to players' faith. In 1990, the New York Giants and San Francisco 49ers each were 10-1 and scheduled to play one another on *Monday Night Football* at Candlestick Park in San Francisco. Pat Richie, the 49ers' chaplain, began pondering a way to use the nation's heightened interest in the game to showcase players' Christian faith, as a means of witnessing. "What if we did something as simple as pray with the New York Giants?" Richie said, explaining his thought process to ESPN.com's Thomas Neumann in a 2015 retrospective on the evolution of the league's post-game prayer circles.

Richie took his idea to the Giants' chaplain Dave Bratton, who already had been considering a similar idea. When they spoke by phone, they agreed to consult their Christian players, who thought a group prayer was a good idea. They discussed a pre-game prayer, but the two chaplains eventually concurred that it would not get much attention before the game, when fans would still be entering the stadium and television cameras would not yet be focused on the field. They opted for a post-game prayer at midfield, allowing the prayer circle to be seen by the crowd and on television.

It was a great game plan, but as game plans are wont to do, this one went awry. Defenses dominated and the Giants won, 7-3, and in the immediate aftermath of an overly aggressive, bruising game, a semi-brawl broke out at midfield, where the prayer circle was in the process of forming. "You want to step in for your teammate," a 49ers offensive tackle, Steve Wallace, told Neumann, "but it's like, 'you guys are trying to fight and we're trying to pray. What is going on?'"

The 49ers players who intended to pray moved closer to the endzone, but did not see any Giants players coming forward to join them. They kneeled in prayer anyway and eventually a few opposing players joined them. The game, incidentally, attracted a record *Monday Night Football* television audience of nearly 42 million viewers, yet they saw only the midfield skirmish and none saw the prayer circle.

At the team owners' meeting in Hawaii in March of 1991, the National Football League reinforced a decades-old rule prohibiting fraternization between players on opposing teams. On-field prayers were allowed so long as they did not include players from opposing teams and "so long as they do it in a somewhat prompt and private fashion," a league spokesman said, according to Neumann's account.

Reggie White, a perennial all-pro defensive end with the Green Bay Packers, and now a Pro Football Hall of Famer, also was a devout Christian and an ordained minister, hence his nickname the Minister of Defense. White vehemently objected to the NFL ruling. "It's the stupidest rule that's ever been implemented," he said in the summer of 1991. "And I think one of the reasons is that they don't want us to pray. And I know we're going to get fined, but we're going to pray anyway."

The NFL, meanwhile, recognized a potential ratings bonanza and scheduled another Giants–49ers game for the first *Monday Night Football* game of the 1991 season, this one at the Giants' home stadium, the Meadowlands, in East Rutherford, New Jersey. It was another defensive effort, the Giants winning again, 16-14.

Afterwards, the 49ers' Wallace saw several Giants players heading to midfield, waiting for 49er players to join them. He was reluctant to join them, though they were looking at him. He began making his way to the locker room. "[But] I had made an oath to myself," he told Neumann, "an oath to God, that I would stand up. So I went out there, and the moment I kneeled, I didn't feel any more pressure."

The television cameras showed the prayer circle, and it did not escape the notice of ABC Sports' men in the broadcast booth, Frank Gifford and Dan Dierdorf.

"By the way, gentlemen," Dierdorf said, "that little grouping we're getting there at midfield, this was supposed to be taboo this year. A prayer."

"I'd hate to be the guy," Gifford, a Christian, replied, "to say that's taboo."

The post-game prayer circles continue to this day, though television cameras tend to be pointed elsewhere. "I think television kind of avoids it a little bit," Len Vanden Bos, the full-time chaplain for the Buffalo Bills, told me. He was sarcastically understating it, I surmised. Television assiduously avoids it.

I wanted to know more about team chaplains and their roles, and

Vanden Bos was gracious to answer my questions. Vanden Bos said he was one of only four fulltime chaplains in the NFL.

"Pretty much every team in the NFL has a chaplain," he said. "Unfortunately there are a lot of really good guys out there who don't have the access I have. I think there are only four of us who are fulltime working for the team that have full access. A lot of guys are kind of tolerated by some of their coaches. Not all the coaches in organizations embrace someone being in the building. We do a lot more than that, for sure.

"If in simple terms I can define the kind of a strategy that I employ, number one it starts with the ownership of the Bills and coach Sean McDermott creating a position for a fulltime person to be here, and then giving me full access to everything. They've set me up with a position where I can build trust with the players because I'm around all the time and not coming in once or twice a week."

The Bills are blessed to have him. This was never more evident than on the night of January 2, 2023, a *Monday Night Football* game in Cincinnati between the Bills and the Cincinnati Bengals. Vanden Bos was on the Bills' sideline, about twenty yards away from Buffalo safety Damar Hamlin, who suddenly collapsed and went into cardiac arrest.

"When Damar went down a lot of us began to pray right away," Vanden Bos told ReligionNews.com's Scott Barkley. "We have a strong core of players and coaches who are followers of Jesus, so that was our immediate reaction. Some guys were praying. Some were crying. A lot of us were in disbelief. We prayed on the field. We prayed in the locker room. We prayed when we got to the hospital."

No doubt many across the country were praying as well and continued to pray in the days ahead. The day after Hamlin collapsed, his prognosis still in doubt, with too many questions and still no answers, ESPN analyst Dan Orlovsky on the network's *NFL Live* show, remarkably and wholly unexpectedly, decided to pray on air, on live television.

"I heard the Buffalo Bills' organization say that we believe in prayer, and maybe this is not the right thing to do, but it's just on my heart and I want to pray for Damar Hamlin right now," Orlovsky said. "I'm going to do it out loud, I'm going to close my eyes and bow my head, and I'm just going to pray for him."

As he began, his colleagues on the set, Laura Rutledge and Marc Spears, each folded their hands and bowed their heads.

"God, we come to you in these moments that we don't understand, that are hard because we believe that you're God and coming to you and praying to you has impact," Orlovsky said. "We're sad. We're angry. We want answers, but some things are unanswerable. We just want to pray, truly come to you and pray for strength for Damar, for healing for Damar, for comfort for Damar. Be with his family to give him them peace. If we believed that prayer didn't work, we wouldn't ask this of you, God. I believe in prayer. We believe in prayer. We lift up Damar Hamlin's name in your name. Amen."

The Holy Spirit works in ways we don't readily understand, but rest assured, he works. Hamlin has recovered, and among those impacted spiritually by his injury and recovery was Buffalo quarterback Josh Allen.

Allen went on *Kyle Brandt's Basement*, a daily podcast, and explained his awakening further, "A kind of spiritual awakening, really, for me," he said. "I know for a lot of other people that maybe didn't have the strongest belief, or wasn't the biggest or strongest Christian followers.

"It's something I've never felt before. It's something I know a lot of my teammates have never felt before, and you can't do anything about it but accept it and lean on your brother and share that moment with them.

"I'll be the first to admit, I haven't been the most devoted Christ-follower in my life. But something got hold of me there, and it was extremely powerful something that, you know, I couldn't deny. It was just spiritual. I was going around my team and saying, 'God's real.' You can't draw that one, write that one up any better."

Josh Allen's testimony is the only evidence necessary for employing team chaplains and for post-game prayer circles, regardless of television deliberately attempting to ignore them. Hall of Fame coach Tony Dungy, a devout and unapologetic Christian, noted via a tweet on January 14, 2023, how God works in those who let him into their lives.

"These comments by Josh Allen prove to me that Romans 8:28 is true – God can use all things – even devastating things – for good. I think Damar Hamlin's injury got a lot of people's attention. I'm praying for Damar's full recovery & and that more people see what Josh saw – That God is real!"

So, yes, remember the Sabbath to keep it holy, as Exodus reminds us, but Sunday games provide unique opportunities for Christian athletes to lead by example, with tens of thousands on hand and potentially millions more watching from home, to demonstrate that the game and its outcome, though obviously important, is secondary to the ability to pay homage to our Lord and Savior, Jesus Christ.

ELEVEN

The Power of One

IT IS NOT A NOVEL CONCEPT, the power of one, how one man or woman can influence another, who can influence another, who can influence another. . . *ad infinitum*. The likelihood was that Tim Tebow, with his "Tebowing," had made an impact on many more than a single child who said he was "Tebowing while chemoing." Tebow, writing "John" on his eye black beneath one eye, and "3:16" beneath his other eye, remains the strongest argument on behalf of the power of one, given the tens of millions of viewers who Googled the Bible verse.

It recalls a popular commencement speech that outlined expertly how the power of one, multiplied many times over, could impact millions. It was delivered by Navy Admiral William H. McRaven, a University of Texas alumnus, to Texas's graduating class of 2014.

"The university's slogan is, 'What starts here changes the world,'" Admiral McRaven said at the outset. "Tonight there are almost 8,000 students graduating from UT. So that great paragon of analytical rigor, Ask.com, says that the average American will meet ten-thousand people in their lifetime. Ten thousand people. That's a lot of folks. But if every one of you changed the lives of just ten people, and each one of those people changed the lives of another ten people and another ten, then in five generations—125 years—the class of 2014 will have changed the lives of 800 million people. *Eight-hundred million people*. Think about it. Over twice the population of the United States. Go one more generation and you can change the entire population of the world—eight billion people."

Yet it needn't begin with one man or woman changing the lives of ten. It can start with one changing the life of one.

John Stonestreet noted this in a piece he wrote for the Colson Center about Tom Phillips, the chairman and chief executive officer of Raytheon. Phillips had shared his Christian faith with Chuck Colson, the special counsel to President Richard Nixon, who eventually was jailed after pleading guilty to obstruction of justice in the Watergate scandal in the early seventies. "I knew Tom had become a Christian, and he seemed so different," Colson had said on the Colson Center's program *Breakpoint*. "I wanted to ask him what had happened. That night he read to me from *Mere Christianity* by C. S. Lewis, particularly a chapter about the great sin that is pride. Tom, that night, told me about encountering Christ in his own life. He didn't realize it, but I was in the depths of deep despair over Watergate, watching the president I had helped for four years flounder in office."

Colson recounted on that program that when he got in his car that night, he began weeping and calling out to God. "I didn't know what to say, I just know I needed Jesus, and He came into my life."

"Colson," Stonestreet wrote, "went on to found Prison Fellowship, the world's largest prison ministry. Through his work in the prisons, untold thousands of prisoners and their families across the world came to Christ. They owe their salvation in part to Phillips' willingness to share the Gospel with Colson. All the great work Colson did for justice reform, and of course the ministry of *Breakpoint* and the Colson Center, not to mention his extraordinarily influential books on Christian worldview, can be traced back to Tom Phillips."

The headline to Stonestreet's story: "Changing a life to change the world: We can all be a Tom Phillips." One man witnessing to one man created a ripple that became a wave and eventually a tsunami.

Christian athletes at the highest levels have a megaphone that most don't have from which to share their faith. They have celebrity, even those who aren't necessarily stars. And with the explosive growth of social media and cable television they have the opportunity to witness to and potentially influence substantially more than ten people, or ten thousand, or even ten million, as Tebow's example proved.

We have this saying displayed in our home: *God doesn't call the qualified, he qualifies the called.* We have witnessed this first-hand in our family. We are humble Christians, my wife Marlene and I, who well into our marriage discovered we were unable to conceive. Tests revealed Marlene had experienced premature ovarian failure. We were devastated. Marlene then asked the doctor, "Do you have any embryos we can adopt?" This was early 1997, when couples had gone through in vitro fertilization, creating a number of embryos, too many of them in many cases. When their families were completed, they often relegated the remaining embryos to frozen storage. Marlene's question to the doctor in the wake of our devastation eventually led to our receiving assurances from Christian leaders that adopting embryos likely was acceptable to God, noting Jeremiah 1:5, that "before I formed you in the womb, I knew you," and to the creation of the Snowflakes Embryo Adoption Program at Nightlight Christian Adoptions. Our daughter Hannah, the first Snowflake baby, was born on December 31, 1998, but eventually thousands more have been born.

The power of one, in this case Marlene, stepping out in faith, asking a simple question, changed the lives of so many Christian families.

Imagine what one Christian athlete in 2023, with the power of celebrity and the platforms available to him or her, can do to help change the world for the better. We bring up once more John 3:16: "For God so loved the world that he gave his only begotten son, that whosoever believeth in him should not perish, but have everlasting life."

This is what in journalism quarters is known as the *nut graf,* the Christian story in a nutshell.

When I spoke with Len Vanden Bos, the chaplain of the Buffalo Bills, I asked him about the power of one as it relates to Christianity, the power of one to influence others.

"That goes back to the Great Commission," he said. "Jesus laid down that model. 'I've spent three-plus years with you guys, teaching you, now you go and disciple other people.' That's the model. You don't have to recreate the wheel. But it has to be intentional. Discipleship has to be intentional. It takes time. Disciple them so they can disciple others.

"I really believe at the center of the target of the mission is these half a dozen guys who I get intentional, one-on-one time with, if I can pour into those guys that the challenge for them is to disciple their children, their wives, to model that. The average career [of an NFL player] is three-and-a-half years. So if you're really intentional with those guys, that is really the center of the mission. That's how we live out the Great Commission. We don't need to figure a different strategy. We just need to be intentional about it."

Billy Graham once said, "One person coming to God for eternal life is worth more than the whole world. Who knows who that person may be in the future? That is the mystery of the gospel. You reach one person and you may reach a whole family or a neighborhood." Or more.

Golden State Warriors guard Steph Curry went to church as a child because he was made to do so by his parents. One of the pastors at his church explained to him that it wasn't sufficient simply appeasing his parents. He needs to embrace Christianity for himself. "I felt a calling, went down to the altar, and gave my life to Christ," Curry told CBN News. "That became the beginning of my own personal journey." One man, witnessing to one child, who became a superstar, who witnesses to tens of thousands, maybe millions, is a perfect example of the power of one.

I know nothing about the sport of cricket other than its enormous popularity elsewhere in the world. But I read about one man who made one decision that changed the lives of thousands and probably tens of thousands. C. T. Studd was a Brit who gained fame as a cricket star while still a teenager in the late nineteenth century. His future was bright and potentially lucrative by the standards of the day. Then in 1883, he heard the renowned American evangelist D. L. Moody speak, and his dormant Christian faith was revived, stronger than ever. "His soul was stirred afresh," Dan Graves wrote at Christianity.com. "Immediately, he began to tell others about Christ. Studd would later say that he had tasted all the pleasures of the world, but none gave him so much pleasure as bringing his first soul to trust in Jesus."

Studd gave up cricket and became a missionary, in China, in India, in Africa. In 1913, he formed the World Evangelical Crusade, now known as WEC International. "If Jesus Christ be God and died for me, then no sacrifice can be too great for me to make for him," he said.

One man, D. L. Moody, touched the heart of one athlete, C. T. Studd, who helped change for the better a significant cross section of the world by introducing Christianity to it, this without radio or television, without the Internet.

This is the power of one. Imagine what one high-profile Christian athlete in the twenty-first century might do, as Tim Tebow has done? Always a good place to end is with the words of Jesus himself:

> *You are the light of the world. A town built on a hill*
> *cannot be hidden. Neither do people light a lamp*
> *and put it under a bowl. Instead they put it on its*
> *stand, and it gives light to everyone in the house.*
> *In the same way, let your light shine before others,*
> *that they may see your good deeds and glorify*
> *your Father in heaven. (Matthew 5:14–16 NIV)*

TWELVE

Seventeen Inches

REGRET GENERALLY INTERESTS me little inasmuch as I cannot rewrite any part of my past, much as I'd have liked to at times. So why dwell on it? As C. S. Lewis so aptly put it, "Has this world been so kind to you that you should leave with regret? There are better things ahead than any we leave behind." Yet I admit to having one regret, a sports figure I wish I had known. He was a man of whom I was aware via my years as a sportswriter in Southern California, but I never encountered him and was unaware at the time of the depth of his Christian faith and his wisdom. He was a remarkable baseball coach and an even better man, by every account. Yet in life he was largely unknown to most sports fans, and no doubt less so in the years since his death in 2009, unfortunately. He deserves to be widely known, remembered, revered, and held up as a beacon of Christian faith, leadership, benevolence, and selflessness to which we all should aspire.

His name is John Scolinos. It is a name worth remembering.

Scolinos was a long-time college baseball coach, first at Pepperdine University, then at Cal Poly Pomona, his teams winning 1,098 games. His Pomona teams won the NCAA Division II national championship three times. He was the pitching coach for the USA in the 1984 Olympic Games. He was inducted into the American Association of Collegiate Baseball Coaches Hall of Fame in 1974, and he was enshrined posthumously in the College Baseball Hall of Fame in 2020, eleven years after his death.

Scolinos was a phenomenal coach, obviously, but more importantly he was a great man of faith, whose steadfast leadership qualities have survived him and are still discussed and resonating today. He did not simply teach baseball, he taught life, and he did so through a Christian lens.

Seventeen inches is the width of home plate. But it also was the subject of an extraordinary speech he gave at a coaches' convention in 1996, a speech that became legendary for the depth of its wisdom and its impact on so many. Pastors have preached sermons about it. In 2016, Dallas Cowboys coach Jason Garrett even made *17"* the team's unofficial motto that season. "Seventeen inches is about accountability," Garrett said. "Accountability to yourself, to your teammates, to the standards we set for our football team."

I wanted to know more, in my exploring the intersection of Christianity and sports, about this man who moved so seamlessly between the two, always keeping his priorities in order, overlayed by more wisdom perhaps than any baseball coach on any level ever had, and the impact he had on so many. These included two long-time Christian friends who helped educate me, Carl Catlin and Tim Mead, and two coaches who are Scolinos disciples, former college baseball coach Andy Lopez, an inductee in the National College Baseball Hall of Fame, and Dennis Rogers, who played for Scolinos at Cal Poly and later served as Scolinos's assistant coach. Their collective reverence for the man they all still call Coach is inspirational.

Carl was an elder in our church in California and had played for Scolinos at Cal Poly Pomona in the seventies. Given our respective love of Jesus specifically, and baseball generally, he has become a treasured friend. Mead, who also attended Cal Poly Pomona, was a journalism major and the sports editor of the college newspaper, and later was an assistant in the California Angels' media relations department when I was on the Angels beat for the *Orange County*

Register in the early eighties. He went on to become vice president communications for the Angels and then the president of the National Baseball Hall of Fame in Cooperstown, New York.

When I talked to Carl about Scolinos, what stood out most was his faith, not surprisingly, given that his faith was always his number one priority. "I can recall calling three or four different times as he got older," Carl said, "and every time I'd call, once he recognized who I was, the first question he would always ask me was, 'How are the kids and are they all saved?' That was just his focus." I am happy to report that I know all three of Carl's daughters and, yes, they are all saved, as are their husbands and children.

Andy Lopez is one of only two coaches to win NCAA Division I baseball national championships at two different universities, Pepperdine and Arizona. The other coach to do so was the late Augie Garrido, an old friend of mine, who won three national championships at the college I attended, Cal State Fullerton, and two more at Texas.

Lopez, the son of parents from Mexico, was raised a Roman Catholic, though by his own admission he was not particularly a good one. "I was involved in some things," he said without elaborating. "God spared me of doing time in jail and possibly prison. If I was caught with what I was doing at twenty-two or twenty-three, I would have been behind bars, not for a long time, but enough to embarrass my family."

At the age of twenty-six, he had an epiphany. He went to a shrine in the family home and "started cussing at that, 'that if you're real you need to show me now.' I had a peace suddenly come over me. He is the God of all comfort. I had a comfort come over me." At that point, he gave his life to Christ, he said.

Lopez's first head coaching job was with Cal State Dominguez Hills, which was in the same conference as Cal Poly Pomona. It was here that his relationship with Scolinos began in earnest. "He did something I'll carry for the rest of my life," he said, "and I even share it with other coaches. I share it with my son [Michael, the pitching coach at the University of New Mexico]. In 1984, my second year at Cal State Dominguez Hills, the program was down. We were kind of bottom feeders of that conference. That was a good conference. Really good baseball. We weren't very good. I had just gotten married. We were playing a game [against Cal Poly Pomona] at Dominguez Hills. They were so much better than we were. I was just trying like crazy to keep my head above water. I think Coach [Scolinos] could see it my face, that I was running myself ragged, recruiting like crazy, doing all these things trying to get the program up to speed. I'll never forget—there was nobody at the game—he grabbed my shoulder and he looked around, looked around, and I'm thinking who's he looking for? There's nobody around. He said, 'Andrew, how's your family?'

"Doing great, Coach."

"How's your faith in the almighty?"

"Coach, it's as strong as ever. It has to be, Coach, because this is a really hard job.'

"Good, because I'm going to give you the secret."

"Thank you, Coach."

"It's all trivial. It's all trivial."

Lopez was taken aback. "I never forgot that," he said. "I went home that day and wrote it in my Bible. Little did I know my career was going to go where it went, and how many times I was in big games, the '94 National Championship game in Omaha, where I was fortunate to win two national titles there, and both times remember sitting in my hotel room the night before the games and really coming to grips with this, that this is all trivial. I want to do a good job. Hell, I want to win them all. That's what you see in John Scolinos. He's saying it's all trivial, Andy. Holy smokes. But when the umpire said play ball, that guy was in to win, he was going to do everything he could to have his team win.

"I had so much respect for the man. He was taking time out of his day to tell a young coach the realities of what it is. At the time I didn't know this, that his wife Helen was fighting cancer and he was taking her to treatments. He really had a crystallized perspective that I didn't have. I was only thirty-two at the time. He was probably in his early to late sixties. He was sharing what he had come to understand. 'I want to win today.' You saw that, that John Scolinos wanted to win that day, but two, three hours before that he had his hand on a young coach and saying, 'It's all trivial, Andy. It's all trivial.'

"Here I am now, sixty-nine years old. I'm in thirteen Halls of Fame, my goodness, and yet I sit around, and if I didn't have my wife, my relationship with my kids and with my Lord and Savior, it would be absolutely nothing. Absolutely *nothing*.

"He was a great, great man. It's hard to put adjectives into what he was and what he meant to young coaches. So much wisdom in baseball and life and my faith. He just had so much wisdom. To anybody who knows God, who knows Christ, the spirit of God is so evident in John Scolinos. Other than my mother and father and couple of pastors I know, I don't know of so godly a man like John."

When I first met Tim Mead, he was virtually fresh out of college and credited another writer, Larry LaRue of the *Long Beach Press-Telegram*, and myself for helping break him in as a public relations flak for a Major League Baseball team. Flattering, yes, but Tim did not need breaking in from a pair of smart-aleck baseball writers. It was evident from the outset that he was a special person about whom I can say unequivocally is one of the finest people I've been privileged to know in my career—a Christian gentleman, genuine, unceasingly friendly, and accommodating.

Mead had been the sports editor of the school's newspaper, the *Poly Post*, when his appreciation for Scolinos and his lifelong friendship with him began to develop. It was mutual for Coach Scolinos. "He revered Tim," Dennis Rogers said. "Coach made Tim feel like he was the general manager of the team. 'Hey, Tim, you're going to go somewhere. You're going to be a big-league guy. I know that.'"

After Coach Scolinos passed, Mead was asked to speak at a gathering at Coach's nephew's house. "I said, 'He's the only man that I know that has disciples on earth. Not followers or fans. Disciples.' I know in today's age people would say, well that's a cult. No. He was so revered. I would probably say Kareem Abdul-Jabbar and Bill Walton were disciples of John Wooden. John Scolinos had a lot of disciples from a belief system and the impact that man had on all of our lives."

The Wooden reference was an appropriate one, given how similar these two giants of their professions were. Both were devoutly Christian men, devoted to their wives and families. Each stood on principle in their approaches to coaching that included discipline and so many other life lessons. Wooden required that his players have no facial hair, no long hair. When UCLA star Bill Walton returned to school once with the start of a beard and his hair too long, Wooden objected. "Coach, if you mean the beard, I think I should be allowed to wear it. It's my right," Walton said.

Wooden queried him on his sincerity, whether that was what he really wanted to do. Walton responded in the affirmative. "Bill," Wooden replied, "I have great respect for individuals who stand up for those things in which they believe. I really do. And the team is going to miss you." Walton quickly got a shave and a haircut.

Coach Wooden also began each year instructing his players on how to wear their uniform properly, starting with their socks.

As for Coach Scolinos? "I'd bring recruits in," his assistant Dennis Rogers said, "and I told them, here's what he's going to say. You're going to have to get a haircut. You're going to have to go class. You're going to have to be respectful to everybody. You're going to have to sit in front. You're going to have to care about the sport, your craft. He's not asking you to win a championship or win a position, but you're going to have to care about your craft, and he's going to give you the tools to do that. You're going to have to be clean shaven and wear your uniform properly."

Coach Scolinos never proselytized, Rogers said, but his faith was at the fore of everything he did in life. He led by example. "Coach never talked about winning. He talked about developing a process and becoming a high-quality human being. Loving your Lord, however ways you do it, and all that. God, family, classroom, baseball, in that order. He had a little chapel in his house where he would pray daily. When he would get to the hotel [on road trips] he would be on the edge of the bed, where he would read his Bible in an upright position, and then he would pray. He would talk about the values of God, but he would never inflict it on anybody else. There was a time to pray, a time to eat, a time to play, a time to take care of your family. He believed it, but more than anything he lived it every day. He was the most selfless human being, the greatest person I ever met in my life. He would give in so many ways. Developing human beings was his greatest gift."

Rogers also called him the greatest speaker ever to take the stage at a coaches' convention, and no doubt those who heard him speak would concur, especially those on hand to witness his speech on seventeen inches. It had to have been his most remarkable and memorable speech, delivered in 1996 at the fifty-second annual American Baseball Coaches Association convention at the Opryland Hotel in Nashville, Tennessee. More than 4,000 baseball coaches on every level—professional, college, high school, youth, even international coaches—were in attendance.

Scolinos was seventy-eight years old at the time and retired. Those in the know had heightened anticipation of hearing Scolinos speak, but Chris Sperry, who would become the long-time head baseball coach at the University of Portland, initially was not among them. "One name, in particular, kept resurfacing, always with the same sentiment," he wrote on his website, SperryBaseballLife.com. 'John Scolinos is here? Oh man, worth every penny of my airfare.'

"Who the hell is John Scolinos? I wondered." Undoubtedly, he was not alone.

When Scolinos took the stage, he was wearing around his neck a chain that held an actual full-sized home plate attached to it. He began his speech and spent more than twenty minutes without even acknowledging the obvious, the dangling home plate. Again, those unfamiliar with him surely wondered about the sanity of this elderly gentleman. But they were intrigued, and the rest of his speech became legendary for the wisdom it imparted and the impact it had on the coaches gathered.

"You're probably all wondering why I'm wearing home plate around my neck," he finally said. "Or maybe you think I escaped from Camarillo State Hospital. No. I may be old, but I'm not crazy. The reason I stand before you today is to share with you baseball people what I've learned in my life, what I've learned about home plate in my seventy-eight years."

He proceeded to ask the Little League coaches in attendance how wide their home plate was. "Seventeen inches," some in the audience noted. He asked the same question of Babe Ruth League coaches, high school coaches, college coaches, and minor league coaches. And what is the width of home plate in the major leagues? The answers all came back the same. "Seventeen inches."

Then he delivered the hammer blow. "What do you suppose a Major League team's management would do if a Big League pitcher couldn't throw a ball over a seventeen-inch plate?" He paused, waiting for a response. None was forthcoming. Finally he said, "They send him down to the minors or fire him. But let me tell you what they would never ever do. They would never say, 'Ah, that's all right, buddy. If you can't throw a baseball over a seventeen-inch target we'll make it bigger for you. Maybe we will widen it to nine-teen or twenty inches so it will be easier for you, and if that's not enough we will make it twenty-five inches wide.'

"Here is a question for each of you. What would you do if your best player consistently showed up late for practice? Or if your team rules forbid facial hair and some of your players starting showing up on game days unshaven? What about if one of your players got caught drinking after hours the night before a game? Would you hold those players accountable or would you widen home plate for them to fit their special needs?

"The problems with most homes in America today, and with many organizations and associations, is there are no standards for people to follow or people willing to enforce them. We no longer teach our children, our players, or our employees, or our members, accountability. It's so much easier for parents, managers, and executive directors to just simply widen the plate. The result is there are no consequences when people today fail to meet standards.

"Let's face it. We have lowered standards in education. Has

widening the plate helped out our schools? We've changed the standards in some religions. Has widening the plate helped our churches? We have lowered the standards all across government. Has widened home plate made our governments better?

"If I am lucky, you will remember one thing from this old coach today. It is this: If we fail to hold ourselves to a higher standard, a standard of what we know to be right, if we fail to hold our spouses and our children to the same standards, if we are unwilling or unable to provide a consequence when they do not meet the standard, and if our schools and churches and our government fail to hold themselves accountable to those they serve, there is but one thing to look forward to."

At that point, he turned the home plate around, so it showed only black. "When we fail to hold ourselves, our children, our players, or our employees accountable to any standards our future gets dark. We have dark days ahead."

The editor and publisher of *Collegiate Baseball Newspaper*, Lou Pavlovich Jr., wrote in a 2022 story, "This giant in the profession influenced more coaches than possibly any skipper has in the history of the game."

Coach Scolinos lived his life in an exemplary Christian fashion, with priorities ordered properly: God, family, classroom, baseball. When Coach's death was imminent, Dennis Rogers was at his bedside. He spoke to Coach, though "he wasn't conscious or anything," he said.

"Coach, when you go to heaven, some of the greatest players in the history of the game will be there," he said. "A couple things. I need to know that you're the head coach. Rod Dedeaux [legendary USC baseball coach] will be the extra coach, whatever team you construct. Because you're going to influence those players in those games you play in heaven."

"You know," Rogers said to me, "how you create something in your mind, sometimes you believe it to be true and sometimes it's true and sometimes it's not? I believe that's when a smile occurred on his face. Two minutes later he passed.

"I still believe that he is a head coach in heaven. I know they all have their hair cut, I know they're wearing their uniform properly, ninety feet is important, pitching is the key to it, getting jumps on ground balls pivotal, come to the ballpark prepared, but once the game is over we'll analyze it and then we're going to forget about it. Not going to dwell on it, but we're going to praise our Lord for the opportunity he has given us."

John Scolinos, long after his passing, continues to serve as a beacon for Christians in sports, a guiding light in the darkness. Strive to win, even hate to lose, but either way, whatever the outcome, remember that in the end it's all trivial. It's all trivial.

THIRTEEN

Coaches, Courts, and Controversies

IT HAS NOT ELUDED me in my decades covering sports that coaches have strong intractable opinions, some expressed more colorfully than others, blue usually the predominant color. When things go sideways for a team, fans are capable of uniting in a chorus of acrimony that can elicit a memorably profane response, as Cubs fans did in 1983. Wrigley Field had not yet installed lights, so they were still playing only day games, including those played mid-week when most fans were working. Those not working, or least not working day shifts, and were attending Cubs games at Wrigley, vociferously let the team know of their dissatisfaction with how they were playing.

After one such day game, Cubs manager Lee Elia exploded, with an expletive-laced tirade directed toward the fans. A popular off-color word in baseball clubhouses was used so frequently by Elia, twenty-three times and with emphasis in his post-game comments, that it elevated this particular tirade to legendary. Even Dodgers manager Tommy Lasorda was blushing. Probably. Again, I am obligated to note that my own language at times through the years has not measured up to the standards to which I aspire. And I have been on the receiving end of profane tirades, most of them from Lasorda. But that's okay. We can't get along with everyone. The counter is that the Angels managers I encountered—Jim Fregosi, Gene Mauch, John McNamara, Buck Rodgers, and Marcel Lachemann—were all quality people with whom I never had an issue.

Some coaches even have a sense of humor. At a retirement party for a popular Southern California sports columnist, John Hall, a colleague and friend, I introduced my wife Marlene to UCLA football coach Terry Donahue, and explained somewhat sheepishly that she was a USC graduate. "We all have our crosses to bear," Coach Donahue responded, smiling.

I note this because it occurred to me many years later that "a cross to bear" is as close as many want coaches to come in publicly acknowledging Christ and Christianity. A coach's expletive-laced tirade, however, is likely to go viral on YouTube and other websites.

Christian coaches who express pro-life positions and participate in pro-life causes bring out critics' venom in barrels. Most Christians inherently understand (or should) that life begins at conception and that all life in whatever stage is worth protecting. The Bible says without ambiguity, "Before I formed you in the womb I knew you, before you were born I set you apart" (Jeremiah 1:5 NIV).

This brings us again to Tony Dungy, a Pro Football Hall of Famer who coached the Indianapolis Colts to a Super Bowl victory in the 2006 season. Dungy is as decent a man as the National Football League has ever had, notwithstanding the opprobrium he has endured because of his faith and uncompromising pro-life stance. In January of 2023, Dungy spoke at the annual March for Life in Washington, D.C., "to support those unborn babies who don't have a voice," he said. This is straight from Proverbs 31:8 (NIV), "Speak up for those who cannot speak for themselves."

This hardly warranted the backlash he received. A headline in the *Washington Post*: "Tony Dungy the regressive and intolerant worst in professional sports." A headline in the U.S. edition of the *Guardian*: "NBC should finally call time on Tony Dungy's amiable right-wing zealotry."

Left-wing zealotry presumably is good with the media "gate-keepers."

There was so much more, as there always is. The vitriol directed toward Dungy was brutal, unfair, and predictable, and yet entirely incapable of deterring him from his mission in life, to profess the gospel and to stand up for those who don't have a voice.

I will now defer my defense of Dungy to the brilliant Robert P. George, the McCormick Professor of Jurisprudence and Director of the James Madison Program in American Ideals and Institutions at Princeton University, and an ardently and eloquent pro-life Christian. I have not met him but have been in contact with him. He wrote a strongly worded pro-life Facebook post about our daughter Hannah (referred to as Hannah S.) that I post here:

A woman named Hannah S. filed an amicus curiae brief in the Dobbs case asking the Supreme Court to reverse Roe v. Wade.

Hannah was conceived by in vitro fertilization and frozen for some years, before being adopted and implanted by the woman who became her birth mother and who, together with her husband, brought her up. Hannah can explain to the Court that she, like the rest of us, was an embryo. That embryoa-Hannah—even when she was frozen, was not something different from the human being she is; on the contrary, that embryo—Hannah—was the human being she is. Indeed, the adult human being she is today was the embryo she was, just as the adult human being she is was the adolescent, child, toddler, and infant she was.

Hannah can explain that just as she was once an adolescent human being, for example, and an infant human being, she was once an embryonic human being. The embryo she was, was not something different from a human being that somehow later "became" a human being. The embryo she was, was the human being she still is, at an earlier stage of human development.

Harry Blackmun, the author of Roe v. Wade, rested his ruling legalizing abortion throughout the United States in significant part on the claim that there is some great mystery or debate about "when life begins" (i.e., when the life of a new human being begins, whether the human embryo is a human life in being). Blackmun was just plain wrong about that. Even in 1973, when Roe was handed down, the basic facts of human embryogenesis and early development were firmly established and widely known. Today, it is frankly ridiculous to treat Blackmun's claim as in the least credible.

Nevertheless, some people insist on claiming that we "don't know" when life begins, or there is some big scientific (or metaphysical, or theological) mystery or debate about it. Joe Biden is one. He says that some people believe that life begins at conception, and he respects that, but he himself doesn't believe it. Evidently, his claim is that there is indeed some mystery or debate.

Did I mention that the claim is ridiculous? Just ask Hannah S.

Our family's respect for Professor George is boundless. He is an exceptionally intelligent man willing to politely debate those with whom he disagrees. Here is what he said about Dungy in the wake of the so-called controversies: "The problem for Tony Dungy haters is that the man knows what he believes and why he believes it. He neither lusts for their approbation nor fears their animosity. They can't intimidate him, nor, in the end, will their cancellation campaign against him succeed. He's bullet proof."

One more defense of Coach Dungy came from Jason Romano, a former ESPN producer now with the Christian sports entity Sports Spectrum, on Twitter: "I've been honored to know @TonyDungy, to interview him, to spend time with him. Maybe you disagree with his faith and I completely understand that. But you can't disagree that he's one of the nicest, kindest humans around, who is consistently giving back and helping others."

Dungy is the exemplar of how Christians should openly and fearlessly live out their faith without regard to criticism, even without responding. As King Solomon wrote, "Do not speak to fools, for they will scorn your prudent words" (Proverbs 23:9 NIV).

Yet sometimes a response is necessary, as in the case of Joseph Kennedy, a Marine Corps veteran of nearly two decades, who in 2008 became an assistant football coach at Bremerton High School in the town of Bremerton, Washington, across Puget Sound from downtown Seattle. At the end of games, Coach Kennedy began kneeling for a private prayer in a public place. Over time, some of Bremerton High's players began joining him in prayer, as did players from the opposing teams.

In hindsight, it was not difficult to see where this was headed in a solidly blue state, my home state, incidentally. It was headed to court. In 2015, Coach Kennedy was suspended, and then his contract was not renewed. He filed a lawsuit with the support of a Christian legal organization, First Liberty Institute, arguing that his praying was a private act of faith.

The case went all the way to the United States Supreme Court, which ruled, six to three, in favor of Coach Kennedy's right to pray anywhere at any time. "The Constitution and the best of our traditions counsel mutual respect and tolerance, not censorship and suppression, for religious and nonreligious views alike," Justice Neil Gorsuch wrote for the majority.

Coach Kennedy also was awarded $1.7 million by the Bremerton School District, and he regained his coaching job.

It is unfortunate that a coach simply kneeling in prayer, not coercing anyone else to join him, had to go to these lengths to protect our right to express our faith wherever and whenever we want in the United States. It is embedded in the First Amendment of the Constitution that states, "Congress shall make no law respecting an establishment of religion, or prohibiting the free exercise thereof."

The attacks will continue anyway, which is why it's so important to defend Christianity. A cliché in sports circles is that "it's a game of inches." Christian athletes and coaches, in defense of their faith, should follow Coach Kennedy's example and never give an inch.

Coach Kennedy's case was a low-profile one, until it reached the Supreme Court, which elevated it to the highest of profiles. Meanwhile, another Christian coach who began with the highest of profiles, University of Michigan football coach Jim Harbaugh, made headlines across the country for voicing his views on abortion. A lifelong practicing Catholic and a vociferous pro-life advocate, Harbaugh, who orders his priorities "faith, then family, then football," spoke at a right to life event in Plymouth, Michigan, a few weeks after the United States Supreme Court announced its decision that returned the abortion issue to states to decide.

The *New York Times*'s headline was innocuous: "Michigan Coach Jim Harbaugh Speaks at Anti-Abortion Event." The subhead, however, let readers know where the story was headed, not that anyone familiar with the *Times*'s political bias needed guidance. It said, "The remarks by Harbaugh, who was quoted as saying, 'I believe in having the courage to let the unborn be born,' run counter to those expressed by the university's interim president."

The obvious response should have been, So what? Universities are supposed to welcome diversity of thought, an increasingly archaic concept, unfortunately. Mary Sue Coleman, the interim president at the university, said of the Supreme Court decision, "I strongly support access to abortion service, and I will do everything in my power as president to ensure we continue to provide this critically important care."

The university, meanwhile, issued a statement: "Jim Harbaugh attended an event and shared his personal views as any citizen has the constitutional right to do. He was sharing his personal beliefs and not speaking on behalf of the university."

His "personal beliefs" were already widely known, and to his credit, he did not back down or back off. Two years earlier, Harbaugh was a podcast guest of Jay Nordlinger of the *National Review,* a conservative-leaning publication. He spoke about the COVID pandemic and God, "and lastly, abortion," he said. "We talk about the sanctity of life, yet we live in a society that aborts babies. There can't be anything more horrendous."

A columnist at *Yahoo Sports* was apparently appalled. "Hearing those comments from him, a college football head coach at one of the most storied programs in the sport's history, is truly stunning," he wrote. "Not only are there more important matters at hand – like the more than 518,000 confirmed cases and 20,100 confirmed deaths due to the coronavirus in the United States, according to the *New York Times* – but the comments are sure to drive a deep wedge between Wolverines fans across the country."

Or not. Two years later, when the Wolverines played Ohio State in Columbus, Ohio, two undefeated teams, Michigan won, 45-23. There was no evidence of "a deep wedge," only euphoria from the Wolverine faithful.

It is inconceivable that a sportswriter for a mainstream national website would have written a Harbaugh column defending the comments that the Yahoo columnist found objectionable. Even had a pro-life Christian sports columnist agreed with Harbaugh, it is doubtful he or she would have done so, or would have been allowed to do so.

Throughout this book, an attempt was made to show how Christian athletes should respond when encountering hostility to their faith, how they should not back down, how they should fearlessly "put on the full armor of God, so that you can take your stand against the devil's schemes" (Ephesians 6:11 NIV), and wield "the sword of the Spirit, which is the word of God" (Ephesians 6:17 NIV). Coach Jim Harbaugh gets it.

So does Dabo Swinney, the football coach of the Clemson Tigers, one of the best programs in the country, who makes Christianity a core component, though not by decree. Nonetheless, Clemson's success with an outspoken Christian at the helm has made it a target for anti-religious groups, among them the Freedom From Religion Foundation. In 2014, it filed a complaint with the university, noting "serious constitutional concerns about how the public university's football program is entangled with religion."

Swinney did not back down, issuing this statement: "Over the past week or two, there has been a lot of discussion of my faith. We have three rules in our program that everybody must follow: (1) players must go to class, (2) they must give a good effort and (3) they must be good citizens. It is as simple as that.

"I have recruited and coached players of many different faiths. Players of any faith or no faith at all are welcome in our program. All we require in the recruitment of any player is that he must be a great player at his position, meet the academic requirements, and have good character. Recruiting is very personal. Recruits and their families want—and deserve—to know who you are as a person, not just what kind of coach you are. I try to be a good example to others, and I work hard to live my life according to my faith. I am proud of the great success we have had in developing good players and good men at Clemson. We win at the highest level and we graduate players who excel on the field and in life because of their time in Death Valley. I want to thank Clemson University and all the people who have reached out to offer their support and encouragement over the past few weeks."

I can't speak for Coach Swinney other than to say that when you recruit players with good character, it is likely that many will have had a Christian foundation.

"I always tell everybody my job is not to save 'em," he said on a conference call with the Fellowship of Christian Athletes, of which former NFL tight end Benjamin Watson was the host. "My job is to win football games. I've come under fire many times from different organizations and things like that because of my faith. They want me to just shut that off and not be a Christian. But God says in Ecclesiastes 3:23, 'Whatever you do, you do it with all your heart, as if you're working for the Lord.'"

Coach Swinney does win football games. His Clemson teams

have won ten games or more in twelve straight seasons, and have won fourteen or more games three times, once going undefeated with fifteen victories. His teams have won two national championships.

Recruits obviously are aware of his faith, yet he continues to field great teams.

Another fearless Christian coach is Jacie Hoyt, the women's basketball coach at Oklahoma State University. Early in her first season in Stillwater, the Cowgirls defeated Baylor in a Big 12 game, after which Hoyt led her team in a post-game prayer in their locker room. "I could feel deep down that I promised I would give God the glory in that moment," she said, "so we're going to pray right now, okay? Because he is working, he is on the move at Oklahoma State right now, and we're going to give it back to him. 'Father God, we just thank you so much for all the great things you're doing in this program right now. Lord, we thank you for this harvest that we continue to reap and feel. I thank you for the love that each of these girls has for one another that they can just overcome really, really hard things because they fight so hard and are using all the gifts you gave to each and every one of us. I thank you for my amazing staff. I thank you for this amazing university that we get to represent. I pray that we can continue to represent, because we're not done. Amen.'"

It was a bold move for a coach at a state university to openly pray with her team, and it reminded me of my conversation with legendary college baseball coach Andy Lopez. I asked him how he avoided getting in trouble with his administration for not hiding his faith with his players. Well, he did not avoid trouble. "Every program I went to I got called in," he said. "By the principal at Mira Costa High School, by the president at Dominguez Hills, my athletic director at Florida, the athletic director at Arizona. All four said, 'Hey, we're getting email, we've got a phone call, that you're sharing your God, your faith.' My desire was to coach, but my desire was to know my Lord and Savior and to share my faith with these young people."

Lopez, like Jacie Hoyt, Tony Dungy, Jim Harbaugh, Dabo Swinney, and Joseph Kennedy are all similar. They are fearless in their faith and backed by the authority of a higher power, higher even than the Constitution. Or athletic directors. As the Bible reminds us, "Be strong and courageous. Do not fear or be in dread of them, for it is the Lord your God who goes with you. He will not leave you or forsake you" (Deuteronomy 31:6 ESV).

Coaches coach, but they also teach, and this is a lesson for all of us.

FOURTEEN

Now Serving. . .

ONE OF THE great pleasures of my life has been the friendship our family has developed with Dr. James Dobson, the founder of Focus on the Family and *Family Talk*, a prolific Christian author, and an uncompromising titan of the faith. We first met him at Focus on the Family headquarters in Colorado Springs, Colorado, in 1997, a long story that I won't get into here. But a friendship between him and our family evolved. Whenever we have met with him, I usually briefly and selfishly have dominated the conversation at the outset by discussing University of Southern California football with him. My interest in college sports was rooted in family connections to the Pacific 12, including my wife Marlene, who graduated from USC with a degree in occupational therapy. Dr. Dobson, meanwhile, had earned his PhD in clinical psychology from USC and for a time was a professor of pediatrics in its school of medicine. He is a diehard Trojans fan specifically and a sports fan generally. *Fight on*, as Trojans say habitually.

I even once asked Dr. Dobson about the basketball legend Pete Maravich, who died in his arms during a break in a pickup basketball game at First Church of the Nazarene in Pasadena, California. Maravich, a Christian, had come to Southern California, before

Focus on the Family had relocated to Colorado Springs, Colorado, to record a broadcast with Dr. Dobson. Decades later, Maravich's death, at forty, remained an emotional subject with him.

We hold Dr. Dobson in the highest regard for so many reasons, his faith and his steadfast defense of the sanctity of human life among them, as well as his general Christian leadership. His legacy is secure, yet what he has said about his legacy speaks to the very definition of the servant's heart.

"My legacy doesn't matter," he once said. "It isn't important that I be remembered. It's important that when I stand before the Lord, he says, 'Well done, good and faithful servant.'" He was quoting Matthew 25:23. Another verse that comes to mind when discussing Dr. Dobson is 2 Timothy 4:7: "I have fought the good fight, I have finished the race, I have kept the faith." Both Bible passages apply to him. Dr. Dobson has been one of those Christian leaders who has epitomized what it means to have a servant's heart, to which all Christians should aspire, be it in ways small or large.

A servant's heart can manifest itself in a variety of ways. Tim Tebow is likely the industry leader in these ways, not surprisingly. The Tim Tebow Foundation's mission statement is "To bring faith, hope and love to those needing a brighter day in their darkest hour of need." Specifically, the foundation homes in on "serving children and sharing God's love. . . by fighting for those who cannot fight for themselves."

Eight different children's programs are supported by the foundation, including orphan care and adoption aid. But his most visible program is the annual Night to Shine that provides "a prom night experience, centered on God's love, for people with special needs." These events are hosted by churches around the world. The participants are treated like royalty, literally, including a crowning ceremony, each one receiving either a crown or a tiara.

I can't know for certain, but it does seem that God gave Tebow only a sufficient amount of athletic ability to have earned him an exceedingly high profile that allows him to publicize his various Christian charities and to raise the financial backing for them. It has given him the opportunity to succeed at his true calling, and it isn't football, but to serve the Lord by helping those in need. This is the essence of the servant's heart.

Two remarkable Christian women and athletes have exemplified a servant's heart in a way that warrants celebrating. Both likely would object, in the manner of the great Bobby Jones calling a penalty on himself and deflecting praise by noting that "you might as well praise a man for not robbing a bank as to praise him for playing by the rules." One of them, Betsy King, is in the World Golf Hall of Fame. The other, So Yeon Ryu, is a South Korean and a contemporary golf star who has been ranked number one in the world.

Betsy King's remarkable LPGA career includes thirty-four victories, six of them in major championships—three in the Nabisco Dinah Shore, two in the U.S. Women's Open, and one in the LPGA Championship. In 1995, she was inducted into the World Golf Hall of Fame. I was privileged to have covered three of her major championship victories, those in the Nabisco Dinah Shore.

Her faith story began in 1980, before her golf season began. King attended a conference, Tee Off in Florida, at a golf resort that provided her the opportunity to practice for the season ahead. "One of the speakers was a man named Bruce Wilkinson," she wrote for LPGA.com, "who spoke eloquently about God's promise through Jesus. At the end of his presentation, Bruce invited those in attendance to accept Christ. I walked the aisle that day and changed my life forever."

In 2006, King made a trip to Africa with a Christian organization called World Vision International that contributed to changing her life even more. She was introduced to the abject poverty in which people were living, including the lack of access to a basic human need, clean water. A year later, King founded Golf Fore Africa, an organization dedicated to providing water wells in areas of need. Golf Fore Africa has built more than 450 wells serving more than 300,000 people, according to its website. It has raised in excess of $15 million dollars to support these endeavors.

King anticipated relaxing in retirement, but instead answered

God's call, as a devout Christian, to assist those in need a half a world away. She exemplifies the servant's heart, a lesson to all Christian athletes and Christians generally.

"As golfers," King wrote for LPGA.com in 2022, "we tend to put a lot of pressure on ourselves to perform. But I know that God loves me the same whether I shoot 68 or 80. That knowledge puts everything else into perspective. I pray for peace and I pray that whatever happens, I represent Christ in a godly fashion in everything that I do."

So Yeon Ryu, meanwhile, is a South Korean who found stardom on the LPGA, winning the U.S. Women's Open in 2011 and the ANA Inspiration (formerly known as the Nabisco Dinah Shore) in 2017. She is charming, well-rounded, grounded, too, whose interests beyond golf include fine wine and food and music. She plays the violin, the flute, and the piano, and once considered a career as a classical musician. She, too, is a Christian, as are many South Koreans, and understands better than most what the apostle Paul wrote: "Each one must give as he has decided in his heart, not reluctantly or under compulsion, for God loves a cheerful giver" (2 Corinthians 9:7 ESV).

Ryu, informed by her Christian faith, is the epitome of a cheerful giver. Steve Eubanks, a college golfer, briefly a club professional, a prolific author, a Christian, and a long-time friend, recounted in a story for LPGA.com in 2020 Ryu's largesse, rooted in her faith.

"In Australia earlier in the year," Steve wrote, "she donated all her earnings from the two ISPS Handa events, including a runner-up finish at the Vic Open, to wildfire relief. When she won the Meijer LPGA Classic in 2018, she made a staggering contribution to the Meijer Food Bank. She has made equally eye-popping donations of money and time to the Marilynn Smith Scholarship and other worthy causes."

That year, she won her country's national championship, the Kia Motors Korean Women's Open Championship. "At her post-round press conference," Eubanks wrote, "the 29-year-old announced that she was donating her entire winner's check, $206,000, to COVID-19 related charities."

Eubanks summed up her generosity with this: "These are not token gifts or tax write-offs. They aren't 'look at me' contributions from a celebrity wanting to appear magnanimous. Ryu does far more in private than the donations she announces to the public. A devout Christian, she sets a servant's example, overwhelming those who know her with her generosity, not just in her gifts, but in her spirit." A servant's heart.

She faithfully lives out her life and faith according to the words of Jesus: "Everyone to whom much was given, of him much will be required" (Luke 12:48 ESV).

A. C. Green similarly does so. Green was a fixture at forward for the Los Angeles Lakers in their "showtime" years, playing alongside Magic Johnson, Kareem Abdul-Jabbar, and James Worthy, among others. Green established an NBA record for most consecutive games played, 1,192. He was known for his Christian faith, for showing up for work every day, for being a reliable teammate, and for remaining celibate until marriage. It was a résumé that, if not unique in the NBA, was close to it. He retired after the 2001 season and married in 2002.

Green was the antithesis of so many NBA players for whom promiscuity was and is a way of life. There are stories of his Lakers' teammates reportedly sending women to Green's hotel room on road trips. They were all turned away. He was mocked for his steadfast abstinence, yet he was undeterred, and he was setting a Christian standard of behavior that he promotes to this day through his A. C. Green Youth Foundation. On its website, under the category of *What We Do,* he includes abstinence. More than twenty years after retirement, the foundation continues to flourish. A. C. Green has a servant's heart, manifesting itself in the kind of role model that everyone should want for their children, its foundation built on his faith. I loved watching Magic Johnson play basketball, but more importantly is watching what A. C. Green continues to do in the community—a daily, weekly, monthly, yearly example of a servant's heart.

In a culture that often seems broken and misguided in the twenty-first century, many Christian athletes are still willing to use the opportunities their skills have provided them to help those less fortunate, while introducing them to the word of God. As the renowned evangelist Dr. David Jeremiah said, "Look for ways to be generous with your time, talent, and treasure. Instead of an instinctive 'No,' learn to say 'Yes' more often. God always returns more than we give."

Ultimately, all of us should do what we can with the gifts God has given us to help bring others to faith, so that we, too, might be worthy of hearing the words to which Dr. Dobson referred, "Well done, good and faithful servant."

FIFTEEN

Applause is Not the Joyful Noise

IT IS A SIMPLE WORD, only three letters, *joy*, but it plays a starring role in Christianity. I do not know how many times the words *joy*, *joyful*, and *rejoice* are mentioned in the Bible, but they do appear with extraordinary frequency, 430 times in the English Standard Version, according to one Google reference. Whatever the number, undoubtedly it is in the hundreds.

The beautiful hymn, "Joy to the World," is a Christmas standard in churches. A song I recall hearing for the first time as a teen at a regional Christian youth gathering in Redlands, California, is titled "Joy, Joy, Joy, Joy." Its lyrics include this verse:

> I've got the joy, joy, joy, joy down in my heart
> Where?
> Down in my heart!
> Where?
> Down in my heart!
> I've got the joy, joy, joy, joy down in my heart
> Down in my heart to stay.

"If you have no joy," Billy Sunday, the nineteenth century

outfielder turned legendary early twentieth century evangelist, once said, "there's a leak in your Christianity somewhere."

I began covering golf in 1985, the year that Bernhard Langer won the first of his two Masters, a victory that began his ascent to eventual enshrinement in the World Golf Hall of Fame. "I won my first Masters, which was my first major, and it was a wonderful feeling but there was still a void there," he told *Columbus (Ohio) Dispatch* sports columnist Rob Oller, writing for Crosswalk.com decades later. "It was almost a feeling of emptiness. Is this all there is? I had lots of money, fast cars, a couple of homes and a young wife. Basically, all you could dream of in this world."

He had everything but the joy to which Billy Sunday was referring.

A week after that first Masters victory, he was in Hilton Head, South Carolina, to play in the Heritage Classic (now the RBC Heritage). At the weekly PGA Tour Bible study, "someone said that we needed to be spiritually born again," Langer told Oller. So he began to read his Bible in earnest and learned that "there it was in black and white. We're saved by grace and not by our own deeds."

He immediately turned his life over to our Lord and Savior. "It usually happens in the greatest time of need and desperation, and with me it was almost the opposite," he said.

I have spoken to Langer about his faith, and it is as genuine as that of any Christian with whom I've ever spoken. In post-victory interviews in his remarkable PGA Tour Champions career, he often casually and seamlessly refers to his faith, as he did when NBC's Jimmy Roberts interviewed him at the trophy presentation in the immediate aftermath of his victory in the 2023 U.S. Senior Open to establish a record for most PGA Tour Champions victories with forty-six. "I was in the zone and praying a lot," he said. "My verse for the week was, 'I can do all things through Christ who strengthens me.'" He cited Philippians 4:13 on national television, earning applause from the Wisconsin crowd on hand. Years before, Langer had found and embraced the joy that a personal relationship with our Lord and Savior fosters, and he did not need to win golf tournaments to spark that joy, though the victory gave him an opportunity to showcase it to the world.

Clemson University football coach Dabo Swinney, meanwhile, is one of those Christians who steadfastly refuses to hide his faith under a bushel, as Jesus instructed when he said, "You are the light of the world. A city set on a hill cannot be hidden. Nor do people light a lamp and put it under a basket, but on a stand, and it gives light to all in the house. In the same way, let your light shine before others, so that they may see your good works and give glory to your Father who is in heaven" (Matthew 5:14–16 NIV).

"Every year I choose a word that God puts on my heart to help me have a specific focus. This year my word is JOY," Swinney wrote in 2022. He noted how he had been blessed with "mountaintop experiences in life" that are secondary to "the climb, the journey, the grind, the relationships along the way, the struggles. Those mountaintop experiences are great but life is about having JOY in the journey. Finding joy and purpose in our day-to-day activities is what it's all about. Just having JOY in the moment. Joy, I believe comes from within. It comes from having the Holy Spirit inside you.

"We can all have J.O.Y. by focusing on Jesus, Others, and then Yourself. This is the perspective God wants us to have daily. Quit worrying about SOMEDAY and find JOY in the journey TODAY. This Is the day the Lord has made. Let us rejoice and be glad in it. God bless."

Coach Swinney's outspokenness on his faith has had its critics in the media, but it has never deterred him. He relentlessly allows his light to shine, one fueled not by winning, though that probably doesn't hurt, but by the joy that comes from a personal relationship with our Lord and Savior.

The best public representation of this kind of joy and its profound influence on a Christian's life came unexpectedly from a news conference in advance of the 2023 NCAA Division 1 softball College World Series, best two-of-three featuring Oklahoma versus Florida State. In the Sooners' portion of the news conference, ESPN's Alex Scarborough asked an excellent question regarding the heightened expectations and mounting pressure on a team riding a fifty-one-game winning streak in pursuit of a third consecutive national championship.

"Talk about keeping the joy of the game," Scarborough said, addressing the three Sooners' players on the dais—senior Grace Lyons and juniors Jayda Coleman and Alyssa Brito. "I'm curious. It's a long season and you've had a target on your back the entire time, the winning streak, being number one a long time. How do you keep the unique pressure that comes with that, how do you keep the joy for so long when anxiety seems like the thing that very easily could set in?"

It was a question they were not necessarily anticipating, yet it produced remarkable answers they could not have scripted:

Lyons: "The only way you can have a joy that doesn't fade away is from the Lord. And any other type of joy is actually happiness that comes from circumstances and outcomes. Joy from the Lord is really the only thing that can keep you motivated and in a good mindset no matter the outcomes. Thankfully we've had a lot of success this year, but even if it was the other way around, joy from the Lord is the only thing that can keep you embracing those memories, those moments, those friendships. That's really the only answer to that, because there's no other way softball can bring you that because of how much failure comes in it and how much of a rollercoaster the game can be."

Coleman: "One-thousand percent agree with Grace Lyons. I went through that my freshman year. I was so happy that we won the College World Series, but I didn't feel joy. I didn't know what to do the next day. I didn't know what to do for the following week. But I didn't feel filled. I had to find Christ in that. I think that is what makes our team so strong is that we're not afraid to lose. Because it's not the end of the world if we do lose. Yes, obviously we worked our butts off and we want to win, but it's not the end of the world because our life is in Christ and that's all that matters."

Brito: "I think a huge thing that we latched onto is eyes up. You guys see us pointing up, but we're really fixing our eyes on Christ. That's something, where like they were saying, you can't find a fulfillment in an outcome, whether it's good or bad. I think that's why we're so steady in what we do and in our love for each other and our love for the game, because we know this game is giving us the opportunity to glorify God. Once we figured that out and that was our purpose and everyone was all in with that it's really changed so much for us. I know myself I've seen so much of growth in myself, once I turned to Jesus and I realized how he had changed my outlook on life, not just softball, but understanding how much I have to live for, and that's living to exemplify the kingdom. I think that brings so much freedom. And I'm sure everyone's story is similar, but we all have those great testimonies that show how awesome it is to play for something bigger. I think that's what brings me so much joy, no matter the outcome. Whether we get a trophy in the end or not, this isn't our home. And I think that's what's amazing about it. We have so much more. We have an eternity of joy with our father and I'm excited about that. Yes, I live in the moment, but I know this isn't my home, and no matter what, my sisters in Christ will be with me in the end when we're with our king."

The video of this interview went viral on Twitter, these brief intelligent and eloquent testimonials from Christian softball players on the best college team in the country, speaking from the heart, and professing the source of their joy—win or lose—that comes from their love of the Lord. In an innocuous and natural manner, they did what the Bible commands us to do, to "let your light shine before others, that they may see your good deeds and glorify your Father in heaven" (Matthew 5:16 NIV).

Winning breeds satisfaction and happiness, of course, but pure joy, as Christians know and understand and revel in it, is rooted in their faith. Golfer Rose Zhang, an LPGA rookie from Orange County, California, exemplifies this, and has done so at such a young age, nineteen.

Zhang's meteoric rise in golf allowed her in her LPGA debut to show the golf world what joy, as Christians define it, means. Zhang was a Stanford sophomore who chose to turn professional after winning a second straight NCAA individual championship. In the spring of 2023, she also had won the Augusta National Women's Amateur. Previously, she had won the U.S. Women's Amateur at seventeen, in 2020, and the U.S. Junior Girls Championship in 2021.

Following her 2023 victory in the NCAA championship, in her professional debut, she won the LPGA's Mizuho America's Open, the first player in seventy-three years to win in her LPGA debut.

She accomplished all this *joyfully*, though it was not success that fueled her joy. In her post-victory news conference at the Mizuho America's Open, she said this:

I grew up in a Christian household, and going into college I really wanted to have an identity outside of golf, because sometimes as an athlete it kind of takes a toll on you if you think that golf is your whole world.

And for me, I realized that being Christian is my identity, and knowing there is a higher power watching over me, and always working to become better as a child of God is something that I've been trying to work on and that I will continue to work on throughout my whole life.

But that's kind of my driving force, just to be faithful, be thankful. I guess be a good presence to those around me. That allows me to go out there and realize that I'm just a vessel just trying to do her own thing. I'm doing it for the glory of God.

A year earlier, Zhang had been baptized at Saddleback Church Lake Forest, the California church founded by Pastor Rick Warren, author of the enormous bestselling book, *The Purpose Driven Life*.

"Thank you to my loved ones and everyone for making this journey possible," Zhang posted on her Instagram account, along with a short video of her baptism. "Being Christian has always been a part of my identity and I'm so blessed to walk alongside Him, proclaiming Jesus Christ as my Lord and Savior. Also, greatly honored to meet and hear from @pastorrickwarren, what a special day!"

Zhang's joy, her infectious *joyfulness*, is not a product of her golf, but of her faith, part of a thread that stitches together Christian athletes, a communion of saints in uniforms, of sorts, whether in victory or defeat, that embodies these words:

> *Make a joyful noise to the LORD, all the earth!*
> *Serve the LORD with gladness!*
> *Come into his presence with singing!*
> *Know that the LORD, he is God!*
> *It is he who made us, and we are his;*
> *we are his people, and the sheep of his pasture.*
> *Enter his gates with thanksgiving,*
> *and his courts with praise!*
> *Give thanks to him; bless his name!*
> *For the LORD is good;*
> *his steadfast love endures forever,*
> *and his faithfulness to all generations.*
> *Psalm 100*

To which all Christians, athletes or otherwise, would respond, *joyfully*, in unison. . .

"Amen."

Notes

6. The Sound-Bite Witness

1. "The 30 Second Elevator Witness," Praise & Proclaim Ministries, last modified 2017, https://praiseandproclaim.com/2017/01/30/the-30-second-elevator-witness/.
2. "Why We Need to Celebrate What Steph Curry Did," Athletes In Action, 2020, https://athletesinaction.org/articles/why-we-need-to-celebrate-what-steph-curry-did/.

8. Mickey Mantle Goes to Heaven

1. "The Legacy of the Last Great Player on the Last Great Team," Vault SI, August 21, 1995, https://vault.si.com/vault/1995/08/21/mickey-mantle-the-legacy-of-the-last-great-player-on-the-last-great-team/.

9. Separation of Church and. . . Sports?

1. Frank Deford, "Religion in Sport," Vault SI, April 19, 1976, https://vault.si.com/vault/1976/04/19/religion-in-sport.

About the Author

John Strege is the author of seven previous books, two of them *New York Times* bestsellers: *Tiger: A Biography of Tiger Woo*ds and *18 Holes with Bing: Golf, Life, and Lessons from Dad*, co-authored with Bing Crosby's son Nathaniel Crosby. Strege's book *When War Played Through: Golf During World War II* won the United States Golf Association's International Book Award in 2005. He has an active baseball writer for twenty years and has worked for *Golf Digest* magazine since 1997. He is a Lifetime Honorary Member of the Baseball Writers Association of America and a member of the Golf Writers Association of America. He and his family live in Colorado.